FAIRY TALES FROM THE SOUTH

First published 1914
This edition published by Lector House in 2023

ISBN: 978-93-5800-742-8

Lector House LLP
Registered Office: H. No. 96, Block C, Tomar Colony,
Burari, Delhi – 110084, India
info@lectorhouse.com
www.lectorhouse.com

FAIRY TALES FROM THE SOUTH

CHARLES AUGUSTUS KINCAID

2023

LECTOR HOUSE

LECTOR HOUSE LLP

"Gave memorial honours to his dead father"

Frontispiece *p.* 48

FAIRY TALES FROM THE SOUTH
OR
DECCAN NURSERY TALES

BY

C. A. KINCAID, C.V.O.
INDIAN CIVIL SERVICE

AUTHOR OF 'THE OUTLAWS OF KATHIAWAR,'
'THE TALE OF THE TULSI PLANT'

ILLUSTRATIONS BY
M. V. DHURANDHAR

TO MY LITTLE SON

DENNIS

WHOSE INTEREST IN THESE STORIES
FIRST INDUCED ME TO OFFER THEM TO THE PUBLIC
THIS LITTLE VOLUME IS AFFECTIONATELY INSCRIBED

PREFACE

These stories first appeared in the *Times of India* newspaper, and my acknowledgments are due to the editor for his courtesy in permitting their publication.

I have translated all of them as literally as possible from the original Marathi. But, owing to the difference between Marathi and English canons of taste, I have had in a very few places slightly to change the sense. In some places, owing to the obscurity of the original text, I have had to amplify the translation. In other places I have had to cut short the descriptions of Hindu rites and ceremonies so as to avoid wearying the English reader.

It may not be out of place to say just a word about the Indian gods mentioned in the stories. It must be remembered that the main Hindu gods are three in number. They are all sprung from a common origin, Brahma, but they are quite separate beings. They do not form a trinity, *i.e.* three in one or one in three. And each of them has a wife and a family. The following genealogical tree will, I hope, help the reader.

Brahma

= the daughters of Agni — Shiva = Parwati — Vishnu = Mahalaxmi — Brahmadev = Saraswati

Kartakswami[1] — Ganpati

Of the above gods, Shiva, his son Kartakswami, and his wife Parwati, Vishnu and his wife Mahalaxmi only are mentioned in the following stories. Besides these, however, the Sun and Moon and the five principal planets obtain a certain amount of worship. The Sun is worshipped every morning by every orthodox Hindu. And Shani or Saturn inspires a wholesome fear, for his glance is supposed to bring ill fortune. Then again, besides the main gods, the world according to Hindu belief, which in this respect closely resembles that of the ancient Greeks, is peopled with Asuras (demons), Devkanya (wood-nymphs), Nag-kanya (the serpent-maidens of Patâla), and Gandharwas (a kind of cherubim). The first three of these find a place in the ensuing fairy tales.

The scientific doctrine is that Shiva is the destroyer and Vishnu the preserver of life, and that Brahmadev is the creative spirit. In practice, however, Brahmadev

[1] For an account of the birth of Kartakswami see *The Tale of the Tulsi Plants* p. 93.

is almost entirely disregarded, while the Hindus worship Shiva, Vishnu, Parwati, or Mahalaxmi just as they feel inclined, or as the particular sect to which they belong requires them.

Lastly, it must be borne in mind that the Hindu year consists of twelve lunar months. In the Deccan the year begins with Chaitra, corresponding roughly with April. The months then succeed each other in the following order: Vaishak, Jesht, Ashad, Shravan, Bhadrapad, Ashwin, Kartih, Margshish, Paush, Mag, Phalgun, Each month begins on the first day of the new moon and is divided into two parts. The first half comprises the period from the new moon to the full moon. This is the bright half of the month. The second half comprises the period from the full moon to the new moon. This is the dark half of the month. The lunar months are made to correspond with the solar year by the interposition of an "adhik" or intercalary month every third year.

C. A. K.

CONTENTS

LIST OF ILLUSTRATIONS

I

THE SUNDAY STORY

When Englishmen and Englishwomen are little boys and girls, they listen with open ears to the tales of Golden-hair and the three Bears, of Cinderella and the Prince, and of the Wolf and Little Red Riding Hood. As the boys and girls grow up, the stories fade gradually from their minds. But a time comes when they have children of their own. And then, to amuse the children, they can find no tales more thrilling than those which fascinated them in their own childhood. Thus the old nursery tales are handed down for centuries from generation to generation. Exactly the same process goes on in India, There, too, when little Indian boys and girls grow up and have little boys and girls of their own, they too tell to wide-eyed audiences the tales which they themselves found so thrilling in their own childhood. Indian nursery tales, it is true, have a more religious tinge than those of Europe, but they are none the less appreciated on that account. The first six stories in this little book purport to explain the connexion between the heavenly bodies and the days of the week. So each day of the week has its separate tale. And all through Shravan or August, probably because it is the wettest month in the year, Deccan mothers tell afresh every week-day that day's story. And little Deccan children listen to the tales as they fall due with the same unvarying attention. For in nurseries, Indian as well as English, tales are loved the better when no longer new, and where the end is well known to, and therefore the better understood by, the tiny round-eyed listeners.

Now this is the tale which is told every Sunday[2] in Shravan: Once upon a time there was a town called Atpat, and in it there lived a poor Brahman. Every day he used to go into the woods to fetch sticks and to cut grass. One day he met there some nymphs and wood-fairies, who said that they were performing holy rites in honour of the sun. He asked, "What are these rites?" They replied, "If we tell you, you will become proud and vain and you will not perform them properly." But the Brahman promised, "No, I shall not become proud or vain and I shall observe the rites you tell me." They then told him that the month of Shravan was coming, and that on the first Sunday of Shravan he was to draw a picture of the sun with red sandal paste, that he was to offer to the drawing flowers and fruit, and that he should continue doing this for six months. Thereafter he should in various ways,

[2] In India days of the week have the same mysterious connexion with the astral bodies that they have in Europe. Aditwar or Raviwar is sun's day (Sunday); Somwar is moon's day (Monday); Mangalwar is Mars' day (mardi); Budhwar is Mercury's day (mercredi); Brihaspatiwar is the day of Diespiter or Jupiter (jeudi); Shukrawar is Venus' day (vendredi); Shaniwar is Saturn's day (Saturday).

which they told him, entertain guests and give alms to the poor.

The Brahman went home and performed the rites to the letter, so that the sun-god was very pleased. Wealth came to the Brahman and he grew richer and richer, and at last the queen of the land sent for him. The poor Brahman began to tremble and shake all over, but the queen said, "Do not shake or tremble, but give your daughters in marriage to our house." The Brahman said, "My daughters are poor; you will make them slaves or maid-servants." "No," said the queen, "I shall not make them slaves or maid-servants; I shall marry one to a king, and one to a minister." The Brahman agreed, and when the month of Margashish, or December, came he gave his two daughters in marriage, one to the king and one to the minister. Immediately after the marriage the Brahman said good-bye to his daughters, and did not see them again for twelve years. Then he visited the elder one, who had married the king. She gave him a wooden stand on which to sit while eating, and water in which to wash his feet, and then said, "Papa, papa, there is pudding to eat, there is water to drink." But the Brahman said, "Before I eat or drink, I must tell you my story." But his daughter said, "Papa, I have no time to listen to your story; the king is going a-hunting, and I must not keep him waiting for his dinner." The Brahman thought this very disrespectful and went off in a great rage to the house of his other daughter, who had married a minister. She welcomed her father and gave him a wooden stand on which to eat, and water to wash his feet, and said, "Papa, papa, here is pudding to eat and here is water to drink." But the Brahman said, "Before I eat or drink I must tell you my story." His daughter said, "Of course, papa, tell it to me, and I shall listen as long as you like." Then she went into an inner room and she fetched six pearls. She took three herself and three she put in her father's hand. And he told her how he had met the nymphs and wood-fairies, who had told him to worship the sun-god, and she listened to it all without missing a syllable. Then the Brahman ate and drank and went back to his own house. His wife asked him about their two daughters. He told her everything and said, "The elder one who would not listen to my story will come to grief."

And so she did. For the king, her husband, took an army into a far country and never came back. But the daughter who had listened to the story lived well and happy. As time went on the undutiful daughter became poorer and poorer, until one day she said to her eldest son, "Go to your aunt's house and beg of her to give you a present, and bring back whatever she gives you." Next Sunday the boy started and went to the village where his aunt lived. Standing by the village tank he called out, "O maids, O slave-girls, whose maids and slave-girls are ye?" They answered, "We are the maids and the slave-girls of the minister." The boy said, "Go and tell the minister's wife that her sister's son is here. Tell her that he is standing by the village tank, that his coat is tattered and that his garments are torn, and ask her to let him come into her house through the back door." The slave-girls took him in through the back door. His aunt had him bathed, and gave him clothes to wear, and food to eat, and drink, and a pumpkin hollowed out and filled with gold coins. As he left, she called to him, "Do not drop it, do not forget it, but take it carefully home." But as the boy went home, the sun-god came disguised as a gardener and stole the pumpkin filled with gold. When the boy reached his mother's house she asked, "Well, my son, what did your aunt give you?" He said, "Fortune gave, but Karma[3] took away; I lost everything my aunt bestowed on me." Next Sunday the second son went and stood by the village tank and called out, "O slave-girls and maid-servants, who is your master?" They said, "Our master is the minister." "Then tell the minister's wife that her nephew is here." He was taken in by the back door. He was bathed and clothed and given food and drink. As he was going, his aunt gave him a hollow stick full of gold coins and said, "Do not drop it, do not forget it, mind it carefully and take it home." On the way the sun-god came in the guise of a cowherd and stole the stick. When the boy got home his mother asked him what he had brought. He said, "Fortune gave, but Karma took away." On the third Sunday a third son went and stood by the village tank. His aunt received him like the others and had him bathed, clothed, and fed. As he was going away, she gave him a hollow cocoa-nut stuffed with gold coins and said, "Do not drop it, do not forget it, but mind it carefully and take it home." On the way back he put down the cocoa-nut on the edge of a well, and it toppled over and fell into the water with a great splash. When he reached his mother's house she asked him what his aunt's present was. He said, "I have lost everything which fortune brought me." On the fourth Sunday the fourth son went. His aunt welcomed him like the others, and had him bathed and fed. When he left she gave him an earthen pot full of gold coins. But the sun-god came in the guise of a kite and snatched the pot away. When the boy reached home his mother asked him whether his aunt had given him anything. He said, "I have lost everything which my aunt gave me." On the fifth Sunday the mother herself got up and went to her sister's village and stood by the tank. The minister's wife took her in through her back door and had her clothed and fed. Then the minister's wife told her that all her trouble had come through not listening to her father's story, and the minister's wife repeated it to her. The king's wife listened to it, and stayed with her sister until the following month of Shravan, or August, when she did fitting worship to the sun.

Instantly good fortune came to her. After years of weary fighting, her husband, the king, at last overcame his enemies, and after taking great wealth from them turned homewards with his army. As he went towards his capital, he passed the village where the minister's wife lived. There he learnt that his queen was with her sister, so he sent for her with a befitting escort. "O auntie, auntie," cried all the queen's little nephews and nieces, "umbrellas have come for you, and horse-tails and guards and foot-soldiers." Every one rushed out to see, and the king and queen greeted each other after years of separation. The sisters gave each other gifts of clothes, and the king and his queen went away together. At the first halting-place the servants cooked the food. The queen filled the king's plate and then her own, and then she thought of the story which her sister had told her. She ordered her servants to go through the neighbouring village and bring in any one who was hungry and too poor to buy food. They found none such in the village, but on the way back they met a starving wood-cutter, and, bringing him to the queen, told him to listen to the tale which she would tell him. The queen brought six pearls. Three she gave to the wood-cutter, and three she kept herself. Then she told him the story of her father and the wood-fairies. The wood-cutter listened

[3] His bad actions in a former life.

with all attention, and as he listened his faggot of wood became all of gold. He went away delighted, promising to worship the sun in the way the wood-fairies had shown to the Brahman.

Next day the cavalcade reached the second halting-place. Food was cooked; the queen filled the king's plate and then her own plate, and again she told her, servants to bring from the neighbouring village any one who was hungry and too poor to buy food. They came upon a petty farmer, whose well had dried up and whose crops had withered. He was sitting sadly by his field when they called him to go with them and listen to the queen's tale. He went with them to the camp. There the queen brought six pearls and gave three of them to the farmer and kept three of them herself. Then she told the story of her father and the wood-fairies. And as the farmer listened, all attention, the water began to pour into the well, and the crop began to look fresh and green. He went away delighted, and promised to worship the sun in the way the wood-fairies had told the Brahman. Next day the cavalcade reached the third halting-place. Food was cooked, and the queen filled the king's plate and then her own plate. Then she told the servants to search in the neighbouring village for any one who was hungry and too poor to buy food. They met an old woman. Her eldest son had been lost in the forest. Her second son had been drowned in a pond. Her third son had died of snake-bite. They told her to come and listen to the queen's story. She went with them, and as she listened, all attention, first the son who had been lost in the forest walked into the camp, next the son who had been drowned in the pond, and last of all the son who had died of a snake-bite. The old woman went away crying with joy, and promising to worship the sun in the way the wood-fairies had instructed the Brahman. Next day the cavalcade reached the fourth halting-place. Food was cooked, and the queen first filled the king's plate and then her own. After dinner she sent her servants as before to bring in some poor and hungry man from the neighbouring village. They found a man whose eyes were so crooked that he could hardly see, who had no arms or legs, and who had not even a name. For he was only known as "Lump of flesh." He was lying on his face, but when they brought him into camp, the queen had him placed on his back and had a jug of water poured over him. Then she took six pearls. Three she kept herself, and three she placed on the stomach of "Lump of flesh." Then she told him the tale of her father and the wood-fairies. He listened, all attention, and as he listened his arms and legs grew out of his body, and hands and feet appeared at the ends of them. He too went away delighted, and he promised to worship the sun in the way the wood-fairies had told the Brahman.

At the end of the next day's march the king and queen reached their home. Food was cooked, and as they sat down to dinner the sun-god himself appeared and joined them at their meal. The king had all the doors flung wide open, and ordered a fresh and far more splendid dinner to be prepared, with any number of dishes, each dish having six separate flavours. When it was served the sun-god and the king began to eat, but in the first mouthful the sun-god found a hair. He got very very angry, and called out, "To what sinful woman does this hair belong?" Then the poor queen remembered that during her twelve years of poverty she had always sat under the eaves combing her hair, and knew that it must have been one of her hairs which had got into the sun-god's food. She begged for mercy, but the sun-god would not forgive her until she had clothed herself in a black blanket, plucked a stick out of the eaves, and had gone outside the town and there thrown the stick and the hair over her left shoulder. Then the sun-god recovered his good-humour, and finished his dinner. And the Brahman, the king and queen, and the wood-cutter and the farmer whose well had dried up, and the old woman who had lost her children, and "Lump of flesh" with the cross eyes, they all remained in the favour of the sun-god and lived happily ever afterwards.

II

THE MONDAY STORY

Once upon a time there was a town called Atpat. In it there lived a very saintly king. One day he formed the wish to fill the shrine of Shiva, the moon-god, with milk up to the ceiling. He consulted his chief minister, and the latter sent a crier through Atpat ordering, under terrible penalties, all the townspeople to bring every Monday all the milk in their houses and offer it to the god Shiva. The townspeople were frightened at the threatened punishments, and the next Monday they brought all the milk in Atpat to Shiva's shrine, not keeping a drop for their calves or even for their children. But although all the milk in Atpat was every Monday poured into Shiva's shrine, it yet did not become full to the ceiling. But one day an old woman came to the shrine. She had done all her housework. She had fed all the children and had bathed all her little daughters-in-law. Then she took a few drops of milk, a little sandal-wood paste, and a few flowers, and half-a-dozen grains of rice and went to worship at Shiva's shrine. She prayed to Shiva, "The little milk that I can offer is not likely to fill your shrine, seeing that all the milk offered by the king could not. Nevertheless I offer the milk with all my heart." She then got up and went back to her house. Then a strange thing happened. Directly the old woman turned her back, the shrine filled with milk right up to the ceiling. The priests ran and told the king, but none of them could say how it happened. The following Monday the king placed a soldier by the door; and again the old woman came and worshipped, and again the shrine filled with milk to the ceiling. The soldier ran and told the king, but could not explain the cause. The third Monday the king himself went and watched by the shrine. From his hiding-place he saw the old woman come up and noticed that the shrine filled with milk immediately after she had worshipped. He ran after her and caught her. The old woman begged the king to spare her life, and this he promised to do if she told the truth. She said, "O King! you ordered all the milk in Atpat to be brought to Shiva's shrine. But what was the result? All the calves began lowing and all the children began crying, because they could get no milk. And all the grown-up people were so worried by the noise that they did not know what to do. Shiva was displeased at this, so He would not let the shrine fill. This, therefore, is what you should do. Let the children and the calves have their milk. Then take whatever is over to the shrine, and it will at once fill up to the ceiling." The king let the old woman go, and had it proclaimed by beat of drum that the townspeople were to bring to the shrine on the following Monday only the milk remaining after the children and the calves had been fed. The townspeople were delighted. The children stopped crying and the calves stopped lowing, and all the milk left by them was brought to Shiva's shrine. The king prayed long and earnestly, and when he looked up he saw that the shrine was full right up to the ceiling. He gave the old woman a handsome present. And she went back to her home, and she did her housework, and then she bathed all her little daughters and all her little daughters-in-law.

III

THE TUESDAY STORY

Once upon a time there was a town called Atpat.[4] In it there lived a bania who had no son. Every day a religious mendicant used to come to his house and call out, "Alms! Alms! In the name of God, give me alms." But when the bania's wife offered him alms he refused them, because she had no children. She told her husband, who advised her to play a trick on the mendicant. She hid behind her door, and as he called out "Alms! alms!" she slipped a gold piece into his wallet. But the mendicant caught her and became very angry. He cursed her and told her that she would always remain without any children. She was terrified and fell at his feet and begged for forgiveness. Then he pitied her and said, "Tell your husband to put on blue clothes, mount a blue horse, and ride into the jungle. He should ride on until he meets a horse. He should then dismount and dig in the ground. He will in the end come to a temple to Parwati. He must pray to her and she will bestow a child on him." When her husband came back she told him what had happened. So he at once put on blue clothes, mounted a blue horse, and rode into the forest. He met the horse, dismounted, and began digging. At last he discovered a temple to Parwati, all of gold, with diamond pillars and a spire made of rubies. Inside was a statue of the goddess, and to it he prayed, saying, "I have houses and cottages, cattle and horses, money and goods of all kinds, but I am very sad because I have no son." The goddess pitied him and asked, "Which will you have, a son who will be good but will die young, or a son who will live long but will be born blind?" The poor bania became greatly perplexed, but at last said, "I choose a son who will be good but will die young," The goddess said, "Very well. Step behind me. There you will find an image of Ganpati. Behind it is a mango tree. Climb upon Ganpati's stomach and pick one mango. Go home and give it to your wife to eat, and your wish will be gratified." Parwati then disappeared. The bania climbed upon Ganpati's stomach and ate as many mangoes as he could. He next filled a large bundle full of mangoes and stepped down. But when he reached the ground he found that there was only one mango in the bundle. He climbed up again and refilled his bundle, but when he stepped down he again found only one mango. This happened three or four times. At last Ganpati got very sore and angry with having his stomach trampled on. So he shouted out, "One mango is all you'll get. So be off home!" The bania was frightened out of his wits and galloped home with his one mango. His wife ate it, and in nine months she presented her husband with a son. When the little boy was eight years old his sacred thread was put on, and

[4] All these stories take place in Atpat town. This literally means "City Splendid." But in the tales it is simply a fabulous city.

his mother said, "It is time to think of his marriage." But the bania said, "I dare not marry him unless he first makes a pilgrimage to Benares." His maternal uncle agreed to take the little boy to Benares.

"It curled itself up inside the earthen jar"

So off they started together, and some days later the uncle and nephew halted at a village where some little girls were playing. One of the little girls said to the other, "You are nothing but a wretched little widow." But the other little girl said, "Oh no! there are never any widows in our family. Mother worships Parwati and so I can never be a widow." The uncle heard this, and thought that if his nephew could only marry a little girl who could not become a widow, he would not die young. So he began to think how he could bring about the marriage. Now it so happened that the little girl was to be married that day. But in the morning the boy to whom she was betrothed fell ill. Her parents were in great trouble, but at last they thought that, rather than postpone the wedding and disappoint all the guests, it would be better to marry their little daughter to the first traveller who passed through the village. So they went to the rest-house to inquire if any one was there. There they found the uncle and nephew, and they married their little girl to the latter that very evening when the cows were homing. They drew on the wall a picture of Shiva and Parwati, and they put the children to bed beneath it. Parwati appeared to the little girl in her sleep. The goddess said, "My child, a snake will come to bite your husband: give it milk to drink. Then put near it a new earthen jar. When the snake has finished drinking, it will enter the earthen jar. Then at once pull off your bodice and stuff it into the jar's mouth. Next morning give the jar to your mother." Next evening everything happened as Parwati had said. The snake came to bite her husband as he slept. But the little girl offered it milk, which it drank. After drinking, it curled itself up inside the earthen jar, and, the moment it did so, the little girl slipped off her bodice and stuffed it into the mouth of the jar. Next morning her husband gave her a ring, and she in exchange gave him a sweet-dish, and he and his uncle continued their journey to Benares. When they had gone, the little girl gave the earthen jar with the snake inside it to her mother. The mother took out the bodice, but instead of a snake a garland lay inside, and the mother put it round her little daughter's neck. Some weeks passed, but neither uncle nor nephew returned. So the little girl's parents grew anxious. The sick boy who was to have been her husband recovered, but she could no longer marry him, and the boy whom she had married had gone away and might never return. In despair the parents built a house, in which they entertained every traveller who passed by, hoping that sooner or later one of the travellers would prove to be their daughter's husband. To all of them the mother gave water; the daughter washed their feet; her brother gave them sandal-wood paste; and her father gave them betel-nut. But it was all in vain; none of the travellers' fingers fitted the ring given to the little girl by her husband, nor could any of them produce the sweet-dish which she had given him in exchange.

In the meantime the uncle and nephew had reached Benares and had given large sums in charity, and had visited all the holy places and had received the blessings of all the Brahmans. One day the little boy, fainted. And in a dream he saw the messenger of Yama, the god of death, come close to him as if to carry him off. Next he saw the goddess Parwati come to his rescue and, after a struggle, drive away Yama's messenger. When the boy woke up he told the dream to his uncle. The latter was overjoyed because he felt certain that now the boy would no longer die young. He told his nephew to get ready, and next day they left Benares. On their way home they passed by the village where the nephew had been married. As they were having breakfast near the village tank, a maid-servant invited them to come to the house which the girl's parents had built for the reception of travellers. At first the uncle declined, but when a palki was sent for them, he and his nephew entered it. When the little girl began to wash her husband's feet, she recognised him. She tried on the ring, which fitted his finger, and he in turn showed her the sweet-dish which she had given him. The parents were as pleased as possible, and they sent a messenger to invite the boy's parents. They came, and the boy's mother threw herself at her daughter-in-law's feet and thanked her for saving her son. Then there was a great feast and everybody was very happy indeed, and at the end they all worshipped Parwati,[5] so she became as pleased as everybody else.

[5] Although Tuesday is really the day of Mars, Mangal, this tale by a popular error connects the day with Mangalgauri or Parwati, Shiva's wife.

IV

THE WEDNESDAY AND THURSDAY STORY

There was once upon a time a town called Atpat. In it there lived a prince who had seven sons and seven daughters-in-law. Every day there used to come to the prince's house two Brahmans, an uncle and a nephew. But when they asked for alms the daughters-in-law sent word that they were too busy to give them any. Some time afterwards the prince lost all his riches and became very poor. The two Brahmans again came to beg, but the elder daughter-in-law said to them, "We are no longer busy, but we have nothing to give you. If we had, we should give it to you." The youngest daughter-in-law, however, was a clever little girl, and she thought to herself, "The Brahmans will get very angry with us. When we had money, we gave them nothing; and now we give them nothing because we have nothing to give." So she fell at the elder Brahman's feet and said, "We have been very wicked and have deserved to become poor. But please forgive us and tell me how we may become rich as we were before." The elder Brahman said, "Every Wednesday and every Thursday you must invite a Brahman to dinner. And if you have no money to pay for the dinner, draw a pair of cow's feet on your money-box. If you want grain for the dinner, draw a pair of cow's feet on your corn-bin. Then worship the feet and welcome the Brahmans. For you will find that you will have money in your box and grain in your corn-bin. And in time you will all get as rich as you were before." The little girl did what the Brahman told her. And whenever she invited Brahmans to dinner, she drew the cow's feet on the cash-box and on the corn-bin, and there was always money and grain sufficient for the meal.

But some days later she fell asleep and dreamt that Budh[6] and Brahaspati came to her bedside and said, "Little girl, little girl, your husband has been made king over a great country. Go to him, and, when you have found him, do not forget to worship us and to give feast to the Brahmans." Then the little girl woke up and she told the other six daughters-in-law. But they were jealous of her, and they became very angry; and they kicked her so often and boxed her ears so hard that she forgot all about drawing the cow's feet on her money-box and on the corn-bin. So she never found any money in the box or any corn in the bin. And every day they became poorer and poorer. First all the men servants ran away, then the male members of the family left, and at last the seven daughters-in-law were left alone in the house. They were starving, but they did not know how to get any food. One day they heard that a king in a neighbouring country wished to construct a tank and was calling for labourers. So they decided to go to the tank and work there

[6] Budh is Mercury; Brahaspati is Jupiter.

just like common coolie women. Now who do you think the king was? He was the youngest son of the prince of Atpat and the husband of the youngest daughter-in-law. When the prince had lost all his money, his youngest son left the house and set off on a journey. As he travelled he came to a city, the king of which had just died without leaving any children or relatives. His subjects did not know how to choose a successor. At last they gave a garland of flowers to a she-elephant and turned it loose. The elephant walked straight to the prince's son and put the garland round his neck. The townspeople were very angry. They snatched away the garland and drove away the prince's son. They again gave the garland to the elephant, but the elephant again put the garland round the neck of the prince's son. The townspeople again snatched away the garland. But when the elephant put it round the young man's neck for the third time, they lifted him high in the air and declared him to be their king. At first he was so pleased at being king that he forgot all about his poor little wife. But one night Budh and Brahaspati appeared to him in a dream and reminded him of her and told him how poor she was. But he could not leave his kingdom to go and look for her. So he thought that he would dig a tank and call together labourers from every quarter. And every day he used to go to the tank and search among the labourers to see if his wife was there. One day he recognised his wife and called her to him. Then they told each other how Budh and Brahaspati had appeared to each of them in a dream. And the king was so delighted at finding his wife that he at once proclaimed her queen of the country.

So the little daughter-in-law was crowned queen, but she did not let the other daughters-in-law who were also working at the tank know of her good fortune. As queen, she gave a great feast to all the workers on the tank. But in her own palace she took some wheat flour, and she kneaded it into shapes resembling human feet and human fists. And when the other daughters-in-law were with the crowd of workers eating at the feast, she went up to them, and to each daughter-in-law who had kicked her she gave a flour foot, and to each daughter-in-law who had struck her with her hands she gave a flour fist. Then the daughters-in-law recognised who the little queen was, and they fell at her feet and begged for her forgiveness. So the little queen forgave them and took them back with her into her husband's palace. And they all lived together happily ever afterwards.

"And fill her lap with wheat cakes and bits of cocoa-nut"

V

THE FRIDAY STORY

Once upon a time there was a town called Atpat. In it there lived a miserably poor Brahman. He had a wife who was as poor as he was. One day she felt her poverty so much that she went to a gossip of hers who lived close by and told her all about her troubles. The neighbour could suggest nothing better than that the poor woman should worship the goddess Shukra or Venus. So she told the Brahman woman to fast every Friday through the month of Shravan. Every Friday evening she should invite a married lady friend to her house. She should bathe her friend's feet. She should give her sweetened milk to drink and fill her lap with wheat cakes and bits of cocoa-nut. She should continue to worship Shukra in this way every Friday for a whole year, and in the end the goddess would certainly do something for her. The Brahman woman thought the advice good, and every Friday she worshipped Shukra and had a married friend to dine with her just as her neighbour had advised her.

Now the Brahman woman had a rich brother living in the same town, who one day invited one thousand Brahmans to dine. At the same time he invited all the townspeople with the single exception of his sister. The poor lady thought that she must have been left out by accident, and that there would be no harm in going, even although uninvited. She put on her silk dining-clothes, and, taking her children with her, went off to the dinner. She seated herself close to her children, and was eating away when her brother came round serving ghee. When he saw his sister he shouted at her, "You have neither nice clothes nor nice jewelry. You have made me a laughing-stock by coming as you have come. I shall not turn you out, but do not come to-morrow."

Next day she did not want to go, but her children, who had enjoyed the previous day's feast, persuaded their mother to take them again to her brother's house. Once more she went and sat down with her children among the rows of feasters. Her brother saw her as before when he came round serving the ghee. He shouted at her, "A beggar woman must, I suppose, act like a village sow, and will not go away although told to. But do not come to-morrow. If you do, I'll have you turned out." Next day, however, she again went with her children to her brother's house. But near the entrance his servants caught her and turned her out before she could eat anything. She went home sad and hungry and prayed to Shukra. Now the goddess had been pleased with her devotion and so took pity on her. She helped the poor woman's husband so that he rapidly acquired great wealth. When her husband had become very rich she asked her brother to dinner. But the brother remembered how he had treated her and was ashamed to accept. He pressed her to dine with him first, and begged so hard that she at last consented. Next day she put on all her jewels and her finest clothes. Her brother gave her a wooden platform to sit on and plates made out of leaves from which to eat her dinner. Before she sat down she took off her gold-embroidered shawl and put it close to her plate. Her brother saw her, but thought she did it because she felt the room hot. She then placed her jewelry on the wooden platform. Her brother thought that she did it because she felt the jewelry heavy. She took a portion of rice and placed it on her necklace. She put a portion of vegetables on her pendant, and a sweet ball she placed on her jewelled star.

Her brother at last asked her, "What are you doing?" She said, "I am giving to the guests whom you really invited." But he did not understand, and asked, "Why do you not begin to eat?" She said, "I have not been invited to this dinner. It was given in honour of my finery and not of me. I had my dinner the day when you gave the feast to the one thousand Brahmans."

The brother felt thoroughly ashamed of himself. He threw himself at his sister's feet and begged for her forgiveness. So she forgave him and sat down to dinner. And the brother in turn went to her house and dined with her. And Shukra was pleased with both sister and brother, and they all lived happily ever afterwards. May I and my readers do the same.

VI

THE SATURDAY STORY

Once upon a time there was a town-called Atpat. In it there lived a poor Brahman who had three daughters-in-law. He rose early even during the rainy season, and every day immediately after his morning meal he used to go to his field with his children and his daughters-in-law. One first Saturday in Shravan he got up as usual and said to the youngest of his daughters-in-law, "To-day is Saturday; you had better stay at home, and although there is very little in the house, you must try to get some sort of a dinner ready. Go upstairs and scrape together all the grain there is in the grain-jars and make bread with it. For vegetables you had better gather grass and make some chutney out of clover leaves." When the Brahman had left, his little daughter-in-law followed his orders as best she could. There was in the jar upstairs only grain for half an ordinary loaf. So she made tiny, tiny loaves and prepared some vegetables out of grass and made some clover chutney. Then she sat down to wait for the family's return from the field. As she did so, Saturn came disguised as a beggar all covered with sores, and cried, "O Lady! I am aching all over: give me hot water to bathe in and oil to rub myself with, and then give me something to eat." The little daughter-in-law felt very sorry for the poor beggar. She went inside and got him a few drops of oil and warmed some water for his bath, and then gave him one of the tiny loaves to eat. The beggar ate it, and then gave her his blessing, saying, "You will never want for anything." He then folded up the leaves from which he had eaten, stuck them into a corner of the eaves, and disappeared.

Shortly afterwards the family came home and found a splendid dinner waiting for them. They said to themselves, "Where did this all come from? There was practically nothing in the house." Next Saturday another daughter-in-law stayed at home. Again Saturn in the guise of a beggar covered with sores came to the house. He asked as before for hot water, oil, and food. But his daughter-in-law said, "I have nothing to give you." The god pressed her, saying, "Give me a little of anything that you have." But the daughter-in-law repeated, "I have nothing." The god replied, "Very well, you will lose that little you have." With this threat he disappeared. But, when the daughter-in-law went upstairs to fetch grain for dinner, she could find nothing in any of the jars. Shortly afterwards the family came home, but there was no dinner for them. So they all got angry with the daughter-in-law, and, although she told them about the beggar, they scolded her harder than ever. A third Saturday came round, and a third daughter-in-law remained at home. Again Saturn came, and the third daughter-in-law behaved just as the second had done. She gave the god neither hot water, oil, nor food. And the god told her that she should lose the little she had. When the family came home there was no dinner for them, and they scolded the third daughter-in-law just as hard as they had scolded the second one.

"And stuck them into a corner of the eaves"

The fourth Saturday it was once more the turn of the youngest daughter-in-law. Again Saturn came in the guise of a beggar covered with sores and asked for hot water, oil, and food. The little daughter-in-law gave them as she had done before, and the god blessed her, saying, "God will make you rich and happy." Then he folded up the leaves from which he had eaten and stuck them into a corner of the eaves. When the little daughter-in-law went upstairs, she saw any amount of grain in the jars, and she prepared a splendid dinner. So when the family came home they were delighted. They could no longer restrain their curiosity, and exclaimed, "Where did all this food come from?" The little daughter-in-law told them about the beggar covered with sores and about his blessing. To test her story, they looked for the folded leaves which he had stuck into a corner of the roof. They found them, but when they pulled them out they were full of pearls and diamonds. Then the old Brahman guessed that the beggar was Saturn in disguise, and he also understood why, when the other two daughters-in-law gave him nothing and were cursed by him, there was nothing for dinner. So they all knelt down and prayed to Saturn, and the god forgave the two-daughters-in-law who had given him nothing. And he was more pleased than ever with the little daughter-in-law who had befriended him. And so they all lived happily ever afterwards. And may Saturn be pleased with us all as he was with the little daughter-in-law.

VII

MAHALAXMI AND THE TWO QUEENS

Once upon a time there was a town called Atpat. In it there lived a king who had two queens. Of one of them he was very fond, but the other one he did not care for. The name of the favoured one was Patmadhavrani, and the name of the unloved one was Chimadevrani. Now the king had an enemy called Nandanbaneshwar. Such a terrible enemy he was too! He could jump into the clouds or dive into the bottom of the ocean. At one moment he would shoot up into heaven. At another he would sink down into hell, and through fear of his enemy, the king had become as dry and as thin as an old bit of stick. One day the king, in despair, assembled all his subjects and ordered them to seek out and kill Nandanbaneshwar. All the subjects said, "Certainly, certainly, O King," and began to search everywhere for Nandanbaneshwar. Now in Atpat there lived a poor woman who had one son. On hearing the orders of the king, he said to her, "Mother, Mother, give me some bread, for I am going out to kill the king's enemy." The old woman said, "Do not be silly; you are only a poor boy, and people will laugh at you. Here, take this bit of bread and go and eat it behind a tree." The boy said, "Very well," and took the bread. But, after taking it, he joined the other villagers and went at their head to seek out and kill Nandanbaneshwar. But when evening fell they had not yet met Nandanbaneshwar, so all the villagers returned home. And when the king heard of their ill-success he was greatly grieved. But the old woman's son stayed in a wood outside the village. And lo and behold! just about midnight the serpent-maidens from Patâla[7] and the wood-nymphs came close to where he was and began to worship Mahalaxmi. The boy was at first terribly frightened, but at last he plucked up courage enough to ask, "Ladies, ladies, what does one gain by worshipping Mahalaxmi?" "Whatever you lose you will find," said the serpent-maidens from Patala; "and whatever you want you will get." The boy resolved that he too would worship Mahalaxmi. And he joined the serpent-maidens from Patâla and the wood-nymphs, and all night long they blew on earthen pots to do the goddess honour; and the woods echoed and re-echoed with the deep-booming noise which they made.[8]

At dawn Mahalaxmi revealed herself, and all of them, the boy included, prostrated themselves before her and asked for her blessing. She first blessed the serpent--maidens from Patâla and then the wood-nymphs. And then she blessed the

[7] For serpent-maidens of Patâla see note to Story XX.

[8] Mahalaxmi is always worshipped in this way. And it is a common practice for anyone who wants anything to blow on a pot and then wish for it.

poor old woman's son and said, "You will get half the kingdom of Atpat and half the king's treasure. He will build you a house as high as his own, and he will give you the name of 'Navalvat' or 'Wonderways.' For this very morning the king's mighty enemy will break his neck and be found lying dead in the king's courtyard," With these words the goddess vanished and flew to Kolhapur,[9] and the old woman's son went home. Now at dawn Queen Patmadhavrani got up and went into the king's courtyard, and there she saw Nandanbaneshwar lying dead from a broken neck. She was overjoyed, and ran back into the palace to tell the king. The king inquired who had killed Nandanbaneshwar. Every one said that the old woman's son must have killed him, because he stayed behind when the others went home. The king sent for the old woman's son. He was very frightened, and when he reached the royal hall he called out, "I have made no false charge against any one. I have done no one any harm. Why, therefore, O King, have you sent for me?" "Do not be afraid," said the king. "My enemy Nandanbaneshwar is dead, and every one says that it is you who killed him. Tell me if this is true." "No, O King," said the boy, "he was killed by the arts of Mahalaxmi." "Where did you meet her?" asked the king. The boy said, "I stayed when the other villagers returned home, and during the night there came the serpent-maidens from Patâla and the wood-nymphs. They taught me how to worship Mahalaxmi. In the morning she revealed herself and promised me that Nandanbaneshwar would be found lying dead, that you would give me half your kingdom and half your treasure, that you would build me a palace as high as your own, and that you would call me Navalvat or Wonderways." The king did as the goddess had foretold. He handed half his provinces and half his treasuries to Wonderways, and built him a palace of which the roof was exactly on the same level as that of his own palace.

When Queen Patmadhavrani heard what had happened, she sent for Wonderways and asked him how to worship Mahalaxmi. And he told her all that he had seen the serpent-maidens of Patâla do, and he also told her on the eighth day of the month of Ashwin[10] to tie on her wrist a thread with sixteen strands in it, and to wear it continually for the rest of the month. When the 8th of Ashwin came, Queen Patmadhavrani dutifully tied round her wrist a thread of sixteen strands, and resolved to wear it every day for the rest of the month. But a day or two later the king came to Queen Patmadhavrani's apartments and began to play saripat[11] with her. As they played he noticed the thread on her wrist and asked what it was. She told him how Wonderways had instructed her to tie it on. But the king got very angry and roared out, "I have in my palace garlands and twine, bracelets, and hobbling-ropes. So throw away that wretched piece of thread. I will not let you wear it." The queen did as she was bid, and, pulling off the thread bracelet, threw it on the floor. Next morning the maids and the slave-girls began to sweep the palace, and among the sweepings one of them noticed the queen's thread bracelet. She picked it up and showed it to Wonderways, and he grew very wroth with Queen Patmadhavrani. He took the thread and at once went with it to the palace of the unloved Queen Chimadevrani. He told her what had happened, and she begged

[9] Kolhapur is the chief seat of the worship of Mahalaxmi.

[10] Ashwin corresponds approximately with October.

[11] A kind of draughts.

him to give the thread to her and to tell her how to worship Mahalaxmi. But he said, "You will grow vain and get so conceited that you will not do what I tell you to do." But she promised that she would obey him in everything. So just as he had told the Queen Patmadhavrani, he told Queen Chimadevrani all the rites which he had seen the serpent-maidens from Patala and the wood-nymphs perform. Everything went on just the same for a whole year. But the next year on the 8th of Ashwin a very strange thing happened. The goddess Mahalaxmi disguised herself as an old beggar-woman and came to Atpat. First she went to the part of the palace where Queen Patmadhavrani lived. But no one there was paying the least honour to the goddess Mahalaxmi, although it was the 8th of Ashwin, and therefore specially sacred to her. Mahalaxmi was dreadfully put out at this, and when she saw Queen Patmadhavrani she said, "Lady, lady, Patmadhavrani, mother of sons, what have you in your house to-day?" The queen replied, "I have nothing in my house to-day." The old woman went on, "Lady, lady, Patmadhavrani, mother of sons, if you give this beggar-woman a little water, you will acquire merit sufficient for all your kingdom." But the queen replied, "Even if I were to give you a copper cauldron of water it would not suffice for all my kingdom." The old woman then said, "Lady, lady, Patmadhavrani, mother of sons, if you give this old beggar-woman a little rice and curds, you will gain enough merit for all your kingdom." The queen replied, "Even if I were to give you a big dinner of nothing but rice and curds, I should not gain enough merit for all my kingdom." Then the old woman got very angry and cursed the queen, saying, "You will become half a frog and half a human being, and you will stand outside your co-wife's bath-room and croak like a frog." But the queen did not mind her the least little bit, and she laughed so loud at the old woman that the noise was like two chains rattling together. Mahalaxmi went off in a great rage and entered Queen Chimadevrani's part of the palace. There she saw all the accessories of worship ready, and there was a beautiful image of Mahalaxmi leaning against the wall; The old woman cried, "Lady, lady, Chimadevrani, mother of sons, what have you in your house to-day?" "To-day," said the queen, "we are worshipping Mahalaxmi." Then the old beggar-woman said, "I am Mahalaxmi." But the queen doubted and asked her, "By what sign shall I know you?" The goddess replied, "In the morning I shall take the shape of a little girl. In the afternoon I shall take that of a young married woman. In the evening I shall become an old hag." After the goddess had taken all three shapes, Queen Chimadevrani called her into the palace and bathed and anointed her. She gave her a silk skirt and a platform to sit upon. Then she sent for Wonderways, and both of them worshipped the old beggar-woman and blew on earthen pots in her honour. The king heard the blowing on the pots and told a sepoy to find out why there was such a noise in Queen Chimadevrani's quarters. The sepoy went there, and when he saw what was happening joined also in the worship. After a little while he went back and told the king. The king said that he would go there too. He followed the sepoy, and Queen Chimadevrani came to the steps and met him and took him upstairs, where both played at saripat until dawn. And all the time Mahalaxmi sat by and watched them. At dawn Queen Chimadevrani asked Mahalaxmi for her blessing. She blessed the queen and said, "The king will take you back with him to the palace, and your co-wife will become half frog, half human being, and will have to croak outside your bath-room while you bathe." But Queen Chimadevrani begged the goddess not to place such a terrible curse on Patmadhavrani. The goddess relented a little, but said, "The king will drive her into the jungle for twelve years." At these words she vanished and flew to Kolhapur. When the sun rose the king placed Queen Chimadevrani in his chariot and drove her to his own part of the palace. He then sent a message to Queen Patmadhavrani asking her to join them. Shortly afterwards Queen Patmadhavrani appeared, dressed all in rags with a skirt round her legs and her hair all unfastened. On her head was a pot full of burning coal, and she began to shout and scream at the top of her voice. The king became very angry and roared out, "Who is this that is shouting and screaming? Is it a ghost or a she-devil or what?" The sepoys replied, "O King, it is neither a ghost nor a she-devil, it is your Queen Patmadhavrani." "Take her into the jungle," roared the king, "and kill her there." Then he went back into the palace and began to live in great happiness with Queen Chimadevrani. But the sepoys took Patmadhavrani into the jungle and told her that they had been ordered to kill her. She began to weep. The sepoys were kind-hearted men and they felt very sorry for her. They said, "Lady, lady, do not weep. We have eaten bread and drunk water at your hands so we cannot kill you. We will leave you here, but you must never come back into the kingdom again." The sepoys left her and returned to Atpat. But the poor queen wandered on until she came to a distant town, where she entered a coppersmith's lane. Therein a coppersmith was making bangles for a beautiful young princess who had just been crowned queen of the city. But suddenly none of the bangles would join. He began to search for the cause, and asked his workmen whether any stranger had come near his house. The workmen looked about and found Queen Patmadhavrani in hiding close by. They told the coppersmith, and he and his men beat her soundly and drove her away. She ran into the lane of some weavers who were weaving a sari for the new queen. Suddenly none of the looms would work. They began looking about to see if any stranger had come. After a little while they found the queen. So they beat her soundly and drove her away. Then she ran out of the town back into the jungle. There she wandered about until she came to the cave of a rishi or sage. The rishi was sitting lost in meditation. But she bided her time, and, when he went to bathe, she slipped into the cave and swept it and neaped it and tidied up all the utensils used by him for worship. Then she slipped out of the cave and ran back into the jungle. This went on every day for twelve years without the rishi showing that he was aware of what she was doing. But in his heart he was really pleased with her. And one day he called out in a loud voice, "Who is it who sweeps and neaps my cave? Whoever she is, let her step forward." The queen stepped into the presence of the rishi and threw herself at his feet and said, "If you promise not to punish me, I shall tell you." The rishi promised, and she told him her story. The rishi took out his magic books and, consulting them, learned that Mahalaxmi had cursed her. So he taught her how to worship Mahalaxmi, and all night long they blew on earthen pots and performed rites in her honour. At dawn she revealed herself and the queen asked her for her blessing. But the goddess was still very angry with the queen. Then the rishi joined her in begging the goddess's pardon, and at last she relented. She said to the queen, "Put under that tree a foot-bath full of water, sandal-wood ointment, plates full of fruit, a stick of camphor, fans made of odorous grasses; and handle them all so that they retain the fragrance of some scent which the king will remember you used. To-morrow the king will come. He will be thirsty. He will send his sepoys to look for water. They will see all your things ready. And when they go back and tell him, he will come himself." Next morning, as the goddess had foretold, the king came. He saw the cool shade of the tree. He was tired with hunting, so he sat down and rested. He washed his feet in the foot-bath. He ate up all the fruit, drank the cold water, and sucked the stick of camphor. When he had rested to his heart's content, he asked the sepoy, "How is it that in the water I drank, in the fruit I took, in the camphor I ate, I noticed a scent which Patmadhavrani always used?" The sepoys replied, "If the king promises to pardon us, we will tell him." The king promised. The sepoys then told him how they had not killed the queen, because they had eaten bread and had drunk water at her hands, but had let her go. The king told them to look and see if she was anywhere about. They searched and searched until they came to the rishi's cave. Then they ran back and told the king. The king rose, and going to the cave did homage to the rishi. The rishi accepted the homage and lectured him at great length. At last he ordered the king to prostrate himself before the queen. The king obeyed, and the rishi handed Patmadhavrani back to his care and blessed both her and her husband. The king put her in his chariot and took her to Atpat. Outside the town the king stopped his chariot and sent for Queen Chimadevrani Chimadevrani bathed and anointed herself, and put on all her silk clothes, her shawls, her embroideries, and her jewels. In front of her she placed all the horn-blowers of Atpat. And as she went to meet the king they blew their very loudest on their horns. The king was amazed when he heard the noise, and roared out, "Who is coming with such pomp and splendour? Is it the serpent-maidens of Patâla or is it the wood-nymphs who live in the heart of the forest?" The sepoys said, "O King, it is neither the serpent-maidens of Patâla nor is it the wood-nymphs who live in the heart of the forest. It is Queen Chimadevrani, who is coming to meet you as you ordered." The king turned to Patmadhavrani and said, "If you had come in this guise to meet me, instead of coming like a mad woman, you would never have suffered as you did." Queen Patmadhavrani said nothing, but sat still in the chariot, and the king lifted Queen Chimadevrani into the chariot, and all three entered the city. And as they entered, the horn-blowers blew so loud that every one was quite deafened. And the king lived from that time forth in perfect happiness with both his wives. And because of his happiness, he ruled so well that his subjects thought that King Ramchandra of Ayodhya had come back to rule over them.

VIII

THE ISLAND PALACE

Once upon a time there was a town called Atpat. In it there lived a Brahman. He had a disciple who used every day to go to the village pond and bathe and worship the god Shiva. On the way he had to walk through the sandy island in the dry bed of the river. And, as he went home across the island, he used to hear a voice cry, "Shall I come? Shall I come? Shall I come?"; but when he looked round he could see no one. The Brahman's disciple at last got so frightened that he withered up until he became as dry and as thin as a bone. At last the Brahman said, "You have no wish to eat or drink; yet you are so thin. What is the reason?" The boy replied, "I neither wish to eat, nor want to eat, nor crave to eat. But I am frightened out of my wits. For whenever I come back from my bath I hear a voice behind me call out, 'Shall I come? Shall I come? Shall I come?'; but when I look round there is no one there." The Brahman said, "Do not be afraid, and when you next hear the voice, do not look behind you, but call out as boldly as you can, 'Come along, come along, come along.'" Next day the disciple went as usual to his bath in the village pond. He worshipped the god Shiva, and as he came home he heard the cry behind him, "Shall I come? Shall I come? Shall I come?" The boy was very frightened, but he did not look behind him. In a short time he mastered his fears, and then in a voice like a bull roaring he cried out, "Come along, come along, come along." At last he reached home, calling all the time and without once looking behind him.

The Brahman looked up as the disciple came in, and he saw that just behind was walking a young girl. He at once married the girl to his disciple and gave them a house to live in close by his own. Now, on the first Monday in the month of Shravan, or August, the disciple got up and said to his wife, "I am going out to worship the god Shiva. But do not wait for me. Just eat your breakfast directly you feel hungry." He went out, and in a little time his wife began to feel hungry. Nevertheless, she knew that, in spite of what her husband had said, she ought not to eat anything while he was worshipping Shiva. So she waited for a little time, but at last she got so terribly hungry that she could not wait any more. So she sat down and cooked her breakfast, and had just put one mouthful into her mouth when her husband came to the outer door. "Wife, wife," he called, "open the door!" Then the little wife got very frightened. She pushed the uneaten breakfast under the bed, got up, washed her hands, and opened the door. She then told her husband that she had waited for him, and she cooked a fresh breakfast, which both ate one after the other. Next Monday exactly the same thing happened. The little wife cooked her breakfast and was just beginning it when her husband came. She then hid her uneaten breakfast under her bed and pretended that she had waited for his return. And on the two following Mondays the naughty little wife deceived her husband in just the same way.

Now on the last Sunday in Shravan, when husband and wife went to lie down, the former noticed a light shining under the bed. He looked to see what it was, and saw several platefuls of jewels. He asked his wife whence they had come. Now they were really the uneaten breakfasts, which the god Shiva had turned into gold and jewels. But the naughty little wife got very frightened and told her husband a bigger story than ever. "They are presents," she said, "from my mother and father and their family." "But where is your father's house?" asked the husband. "It is in the sandy island," said the little wife, "which lies in the dry bed of the river." "You must take me there," said her husband. Next morning they started off together. And the naughty little wife could hardly walk, she was so frightened. For she knew quite well that her father had no house in the sandy island. But on the way she prayed to Shiva, "Please, please, god Shiva, create a house for my father in the sandy island which lies in the dry bed of the river, even if it be only for half an hour."

At last the husband and wife came to the sandy island. And there, lo and behold! they saw a great big palace, and a splendidly dressed young man came forward and greeted the disciple as his brother-in-law. And a handsome old knight came forward and greeted the disciple as his son-in-law. And a beautiful young woman greeted the naughty little wife as the sister of her husband. And a lovely little girl ran up and embraced her and called her "sister." And slave girls and maid-servants ran forward to offer her their service. A guard of soldiers kept watch by the palace, and at the door there were sentries, who made way for them as they passed. Inside the house the little wife and her husband were given platforms to sit upon, and a splendid feast was all ready prepared for them to eat. After they had feasted, they got up and said good-bye to the little wife's father and mother, and garlands of flowers were placed round their necks, and they started for their home. When they had gone half-way, the naughty little wife remembered that she had hung her garland on a peg and had forgotten to bring it with her. So she and her husband went back to the sandy island. But when they got there, there was no palace, there were no soldiers to guard it, there were no sentries at the door, there were no maid-servants nor slave girls. There was nothing there but just a sandy island in the middle of a dry river-bed. And on the sand lay the garland which the naughty little wife had forgotten. She took it up and put it round her neck.

But her husband asked her, "What has happened to your father's house?" The naughty little wife replied, all in tears, "As it came, so it went. But if you promise to forgive me, I shall tell you." The husband promised. So she told him how every Monday she had felt so hungry and how she had cooked her breakfast, and then, on hearing her husband's voice, had pushed it under their bed. She also told him that the god Shiva had turned the food into gold and jewels. "Then when you asked me," she went on, "I felt so frightened that I said they were presents from my father and mother and the rest of my family. And when you made me take you to my father's house, I prayed the god Shiva to create, if only for half an hour, a house for my father on the sandy island in the dry river-bed. And he graciously granted my request." Then the husband forgave the naughty little wife. And she became quite good and never told him any more stories. And they both went home and lived happily ever afterwards.

IX

NAGOBA, THE SNAKE-KING

Once upon a time there was a town called Atpat. In it there lived a Brahman who had seven little daughters-in-law. In the fulness of time the month of Shravan came and with it Nagpanchmi Day[12]. In honour of the festival, one little daughter-in-law went to her grandpapa's house, another went to her great grandpapa's house, another went to her father's house, until at last only the youngest daughter-in-law remained behind. Her father and mother were dead, and she had no uncles and no aunts and no little brothers or sisters. So the poor little daughter-in-law felt very sad and sat down and cried in a corner. Then she remembered that it was Nagpanchmi Day, and that it was a festival in honour of Nagoba, the great snake-king. So she prayed under her breath, "Please, please, snake-king, come and pretend that you have been sent to fetch me to my father's house!" And the great snake-king heard the prayer and felt quite sorry for the poor little daughter-in-law who was crying in the corner. He assumed the guise of a Brahman and came to the house where the little daughter-in-law was, and said that he had been sent to fetch her to her father's house. Her father-in-law was very much astonished. For he wondered why, if the new-comer really was a relative of the little daughter-in-law, he had never paid him a visit before. At last he asked the little daughter-in-law who the new-comer was. She did not know in the least. But she was so overjoyed that some one should have come for her that she at once answered, "He is my mother's brother." Her father-in-law believed her and sent her off in the care of Nagoba, the snake-king. Still disguised as a Brahman, he took her to the entrance of his underground palace and there he told her who he was. He then reassumed his true appearance, and, expanding the mighty hood behind his head, he seated the little girl on it and took her down to his splendid dwelling-house beneath the earth. In the central hall he presented her to the snake-queen and to all the snake-princes, and told them that in no circumstances whatever were they to bite the little daughter-in-law.

One day the snake-queen was about to be confined. So she asked the little daughter-in-law to sit by her side with the lamp in her hand. The little daughter-in-law did so, and a little time afterwards the snake-queen gave birth to a fresh litter of little snake-princes. When the little daughter-in-law saw them all wriggling about, she was frightened out of her wits. She let the lamp slip out of her hands.

[12] Nagpanchmi Day falls on Shravan Sud 5, *i.e.* the 5th day of the bright half of Shravan.

It fell on the ground and burnt all the little snakes' tails off. The snake-queen did her best to comfort them, but the stumps of the little princes' tails ached so dreadfully that it was ever so long before the snake-queen could put them off to sleep. When the snake-king came home that evening, she told him what had happened. And she was so cross with the little daughter-in-law, that the snake-king had to promise that she should go back to her father-in-law's house. A few days later, the snake-king assumed once again the guise of a Brahman, and, loading the little daughter-in-law with presents, took her back to her husband's home. In the course of time the little snake-princes grew up, but their tails never grew again. So their father, the snake-king, called one little prince, No-tail; and the second little prince, Cut-tail; and the third little prince, Dock-tail. And one day they asked the snake-queen how it was that their tails had been broken off. She told them how the little daughter-in-law had burnt them off by dropping the lamp on them.

The snake-princes, when they heard their mother's answer, were terribly cross with the little daughter-in-law, and they vowed that they would be revenged on her. So they found out where she lived, and they sent a message to her house, saying that they were coming to pay her a visit. But they really meant to bite her to death directly they saw her. The little daughter-in-law was overjoyed when she heard that the snake-princes were coming to visit her. For ever since the snake-king had pretended to be her uncle, she always thought of little No-tail and little Cut-tail and little Dock-tail as if they had been her own cousins. Now it so happened that the very day on which they were expected at the little daughter-in-law's house was Nagpanchmi Day. The little daughter-in-law was sitting in the house all alone waiting for little Prince No-tail, little Prince Cut-tail, and little Prince Dock-tail. They were late in coming, so to pass the time she drew pictures of Nagoba, the snake-king, on her dining-platform and on the wall. When she had finished the pictures, she worshipped them and offered them milk and food. Then she prayed to the great snake-king, "Please please, King Nagoba, guard from all hurt, wherever they may be, my little cousins No-tail and Cut-tail and Dock-tail." And last of all she prostrated herself at full length before the pictures which she had drawn on the wall and on her dining-platform.

In the meantime little Prince No-tail and little Prince Cut-tail and little Prince Dock-tail had come up without the little daughter-in-law noticing them. But when they saw the honour which she was paying their father, King Nagoba, and heard the prayer which she had offered on their behalf, they no longer wished to kill or bite the little daughter-in-law. On the contrary, they made themselves known to her and stayed all that day in the house and were as good and as nice as possible. When night fell, they drank the milk which she had offered to the snake-king. And in its place they put a necklace with nine beautiful jewels in it. Before day broke they went away quietly and returned to their father's palace under the ground. Next morning when the little daughter-in-law woke up she saw the lovely necklace lying where the milk had been. She gave a shout of delight, and putting it round her neck, she ran all over the house showing it to everybody. And every one was perfectly charmed with it. And the snake-princes never again came to bite any one in that household. And the little daughter-in-law and her husband and her father-in-law and little Prince No-tail and little Prince Cut-tail and little Prince Dock-tail, they all lived happily for ever so long afterwards.

"They no longer wished to kill or bite the little daughter-in-law"

X

PARWATI AND THE BEGGAR-MAN

Once upon a time there was a town called Atpat. In It there lived a Brahman. He had seven daughters, and when they had reached a marriageable age he asked them who would arrange their marriages and bring them handsome husbands and make their fortunes. The six eldest daughters said, "Papa, Papa, you of course. You will arrange our marriages and bring us handsome husbands and make our fortunes for us." But the youngest daughter was a naughty little girl. She got into a temper all about nothing, and she stamped her foot, and she turned her back on her father and said, "I will arrange my own marriage, and I will get a handsome husband for myself, and I will make my fortune myself." The Brahman was very angry with her, and so how do you think he punished her? He first searched about and found six rich and handsome boys. Then he married them with great pomp and display to his six eldest daughters. But the youngest girl he gave in marriage to a miserable beggar-man. You never saw such a beggar-man as he was! There was not a spot on his skin that was not black with leprosy, and his feet and hands had rotted right off. If you had seen him you would have said, "If that beggar-man does not die to-day he will certainly die to-morrow. For he cannot possibly live any longer!" When the marriage was celebrated, the little girl's mother filled her lap with pulse and then handed her over to the beggar-man to see what sort of fortune would be hers. But in a few days the beggar-man died. His corpse was taken to the burning-ground, and his little widow followed it. But when his relatives wanted to burn the body, she forbade them and told them to go away. For she said, "My fortune is still to come, whatever it may be." They all got round her and tried to persuade her that there was no use in her staying by the corpse, but she would not mind what they said. At last they were quite tired out and went home, leaving her in the burning-ground. When they had gone she took her husband's corpse on to her lap. Then she prayed to the god Shiva and said:

> "My parents disown me. O why was I born
> Both as orphan and widow to live all forlorn?"

As she prayed, she put the pulse which her mother had put into her lap grain by grain in the dead man's mouth. Then she sat there crying until midnight. Now it happened that on that very night Shiva and Parwati were in their chariot driving through the air over that very place. Parwati said suddenly to her husband, "I hear a woman crying, let us go and see what it is." The god Shiva drove his chariot down to earth. He and Parwati got out and saw the Brahman's youngest daughter crying. They asked her what the reason was, and she told them. Then Parwati pitied her and said, "Your aunt has acquired great merit by her piety and devotions. You go to her and get her to give you all her merit and so you will bring your husband back to life." The god Shiva and Parwati then mounted on their chariot and disappeared. Next morning the little widow left her husband's body, went to her aunt's house and begged her to give her all the merit which she had acquired, and told her the cause of the request. The aunt was very good and gave her all her own merit. The little widow then went back to the burning-ground and with its aid brought her husband back to life. But this time he was no longer a beggar-man black with leprosy and with feet and hands that had rotted away. He was a beautiful young man with well-shaped feet and a beautiful fair skin, and the little widow took her husband back to her father's house. "Papa, Papa," she said, "you turned me out, but the gods have brought me back, and good fortune came to me without your bringing it." The father was too frightened of Parwati to say anything, so he held his peace. And the little girl and her husband, the beggar-man, lived happily ever afterwards.

"They asked her what the reason was, and she told them"

XI

PARWATI AND THE BRAHMAN

Once upon a time there was a town called Atpat. In it there lived a poor Brahman. When the month of Bhadrapad came round, every household bought little images of Parwati, and the women began to walk about the streets and sound gongs. When the poor Brahman's children saw this they went home and said to their mother, "Mummy, Mummy, please buy us little images of Parwati like the other little boys and girls have." But their mother said, "What is the use of my buying images of Parwati? If I do we shall have to make offerings, and there is absolutely nothing in the house. You run to papa and tell him to go into the bazaar and buy grain. If he buys grain I'll buy you images of Parwati." The children got up and ran to their father and cried out, "Papa, Papa, Mama says that she will buy us images of Parwati if you will go into the bazaar and get food to offer to them." Their father at first searched all over the house but could find no grain. And then he looked in his purse but he could find no money with which to go to the bazaar and buy grain. But although he tried to explain this to his children, they would not listen to him. They screamed at him and shouted, "Papa, Papa, Mummy says that she will buy us images of Parwati if you will get food to offer to them." "Papa, Papa, why should we not have images of Parwati like the other little boys and girls." At last they bothered the poor Brahman so much that he felt worried to death. "I love," he said, "my children as if they were made of gold, but they will not mind what I say. They will not understand that it is nothing but poverty which prevents my buying food and offering it to Parwati. I might go out and beg, but when I do, no one ever gives me anything. Death is better than a life like this." With these words he got up and walked to the edge of the village pond and determined to drown himself. It was dark when he started, and half-way he met an old woman. She heard him coming and asked him who he was. He told her all his trouble, and said that he meant to jump into the pond to escape from his children. The woman comforted him and prevailed on him to turn home again. He took her home. His wife came to the door with a lamp and asked who she was. The husband did not like to say that he had only just met her on the road, so he said to his wife, "She is my grandmother." The wife thereupon welcomed her and invited her to come in and stay to supper. But her heart felt as heavy as lead, for she knew that there was nothing to eat inside the house. When the old woman had seated herself inside the house, the Brahman's wife got up and, in despair, went to look inside the grain-pots. She knew they were empty, but she thought that she would first look into them once again. But, lo and behold! when she looked this time she found the grain-pots brimming over with grain. She called her husband, and they were both perfectly delighted. And the wife prepared bowls full of rice-gruel, and every one, children and all, ate the rice-gruel till the skins on their stomachs felt quite tight. And they went to bed as happy as possible. Next morning the old woman called to the Brahman, "My son, my son, get me water for my bath and cook me a nice hot dinner, and please be quick about it, and do not start making objections." The Brahman got up and called his wife, and they got water for the old woman's bath, and then the Brahman went out to beg. When he had gone out before, no one had ever given him anything. But to-day every one ran out and gave him food and molasses and copper coins. Then he went back home in splendid spirits. His wife prepared a glorious dinner, and the children ate so much that the skin on their stomachs felt as tight as a kettle-drum. After breakfast the old woman said to the Brahman, "To-morrow I want a milk-pudding for dinner." "But, Grandmamma," said the Brahman, "where shall I get the milk from?" The old woman said, "Don't worry about that. Just get up and hammer down as many pegs as you can in your courtyard. Then this evening, when the cattle come home, call to the village cows and buffaloes by name, and they will come to you, and if you milk them you will get enough milk for my pudding to-morrow." The Brahman did as the old woman ordered him, and that evening he called to the cows and buffaloes by name to come to his courtyard. And from every direction the cows and buffaloes came running up. And behind them galloped all the little calves with their heels in the air and their tails stuck out straight behind them. At last the Brahman's courtyard was filled so full that no more cows or buffaloes could enter. And he milked them all, and next day his wife cooked a milk-pudding such as one would not see again if one lived a thousand years. And the children ate until they were so tired of eating that they just rolled over and went fast asleep. But that evening the old woman said, "My son, my son, I want you to take me home." "But, Grandmamma, Grandmamma," said the Brahman, "how can I take you home, for I have had all this good luck only because of you. Directly you go away my good luck will vanish." "Do not be afraid," said the old woman, "for I am Parwati. If I bless you your good luck will never vanish. Therefore you must come with me and see me home." But the Brahman said, "I do not want my good luck only to continue. I want it to increase." The old woman said, "If you come with me I shall give you some sand. When you go back home, scatter it all over the house and over your jars and your pots, and put it inside your boxes and your cupboards, and scatter it all over your courtyard too, and you will find that your good luck will never be any less than it is now." The Brahman was satisfied with this. He worshipped the old woman and went with her towards the tank until she suddenly disappeared. He returned home and scattered sand all over his house and over his jars and his pots and inside his boxes and his cupboards, and from that day on, his good luck never left him. And his wealth increased, and his children increased. And they all lived happily ever afterwards.

XII

SOMA, THE WASHERWOMAN

Once upon a time there was a town called Atpat. In it there lived a poor Brahman who had seven sons and seven daughters-in-law. He had also one daughter called Gunvanti and a wife called Dhanvanti. Whenever a mendicant Brahman came to this house, it was the custom of all the ladies to give him alms and then prostrate themselves in front of him. One day a Brahman came, tall as a tree and shining like the sun. The seven daughters-in-law ran out as usual and gave him alms and then threw themselves at full length at his feet. The Brahman blessed them and said, "Increase of children be yours; increase of wealth be yours; may your husbands cherish you all your lives." But the Brahman's daughter Gunvanti was a lazy little girl, and when the mendicant came she was still in bed. Her mother, Dhanvanti, rushed into her room and cried, "Daughter, daughter, get up and give the Brahman alms," The little girl jumped up in a fright and ran out and put alms before him and prostrated herself at his feet. The mendicant blessed her and said, "Observe the precepts of religion."

The little girl ran back to her mother. "Mother, Mother," she cried, "Bhatji[13] did not give me the same blessing as he gave to my sisters-in-law," Her mother said, "Go back again and give him some more alms and see what he does," The little girl ran back, put some more alms before the mendicant, and again prostrating herself asked for his blessing. Once more he said, "Observe the precepts of religion," Then Dhanvanti asked him why he gave her daughter such a strange blessing. The mendicant replied, "Because widowhood will come upon her immediately after her marriage," Dhanvanti threw herself before the Brahman and grasped his feet and cried, weeping, "Tell me how I may escape this evil; what shall I do to save my one little girl from becoming a widow?" The Brahman pitied her and said, "Lady, lady, do not weep; I shall give you a remedy by which to cure this evil. Across the seven seas there is an island. In it there lives a washerwoman called Soma. If you can fetch her to your daughter's wedding, she will escape the evil that threatens her. When the wedding is over, you must send Soma back with all honour to her house." With these words the mendicant took up his wallet and went to collect alms elsewhere. When her husband returned home Dhanvanti told him what had happened. "Some one," she added, "must go across the seven seas, to fetch Soma, the washerwoman." The father and mother called up their sons and said, "Those of you who honour your parents will take your sister and cross the seven seas to bring Soma here." But all the sons turned to their mother and

[13] Bhatji is the name by which a mendicant Brahman is addressed.

said, "All you care about is your daughter. You do not love us the least little bit. So we shall not cross the seven seas and bring Soma here just on her account." The mother began to cry, and the father got very cross. He turned to his wife and said, "From henceforth you have no sons. To me our seven sons are as if they had never been born. But do not get frightened about our little girl I myself shall cross the seven seas and fetch Soma, the washerwoman." Then the youngest of the seven sons said to his father, "Daddy, Daddy, you must not say that you have no sons when here we are, all seven of us. I shall take my sister Gunvanti with me, and we shall go and fetch Soma, the washerwoman." A few days later the two children prostrated themselves before their parents and began their voyage.

In course of time they came to the seashore. But the wind was blowing, the waves were rolling in, and the foam was splashing over the rocks. The brother and sister could not imagine how they were to continue their journey. There was no one near to give them food, there was no one near to give them drink, and they could think of nothing better than to lie down and die. But they first resolved to pray to the god Shiva, "Please, please, God Shiva," prayed the two children, "get us out of this terrible trouble." After praying they went and sat under a banian tree, and all day long they had nothing to eat or drink. Now on the very top of the banian tree was an eagle's nest, and in it there were several little eagles. When evening came, father eagle and mother eagle came home and began to feed their young. But the little eagles would not eat anything at all. Mother eagle said, "Children, children, what is the matter?" "O Mummy, Mummy," cried the little eagles, "two strangers have come to our house, and they are sitting under our tree, and they have had nothing to eat all day!" Father eagle and mother eagle flew to the ground and began to ask the boy what his trouble was. "Do not be frightened," said father eagle; "whatever your business, I'll help you to get it done. Do not go to bed without supper. I'll bring you some fruit. Eat some of it yourself and give the rest to your little sister."

The boy told father eagle what had happened, and how it was that they had to cross the seven seas. Father eagle said, "I shall carry you both across directly you wake up to-morrow, and I shall put you down at Soma the washerwoman's door." Then the two children felt very happy and thanked the god Shiva. And after eating father eagle's fruit, they lay down under the tree and fell fast asleep in no time. Next morning father eagle and mother eagle came down the tree, and father eagle took the boy on his back, and mother eagle took the girl on her back, and off they flew across the seven seas. The wind blew, and the waves rolled mountains high, and the foam splashed over the rocks. But father eagle and mother eagle flew straight on until they came to the door of Soma, the washerwoman. There they left the boy and girl and went back to the tree where the little eagles were waiting for them. The boy and girl were too frightened to walk into Soma's house, so they hid all that day, and next morning they got up at dawn and they swept the courtyard and neaped the floor with cow-dung. And then, before any one could see them, they ran away and hid. And this they did every day for a whole year.

At last Soma one day called all her children and all her little daughters-in-law and said, "Who among you gets up so early? Who sweeps my courtyard? Who clears my floor?" All the children and all the little daughters-in-law said, "It is not I," "It is not I," "It is not I." Then Soma became very curious to know who it was. So the following night she did not go to bed. She sat up, but nothing happened until just after dawn. Then she saw the little Brahman girl sweeping the courtyard and her brother cleaning the floor. Soma got up and said, "Children, who are you?" They replied, "We are Brahmans." "But I am only a washerwoman," said Soma; "I am a low-caste woman, why do you sweep my courtyard and neap my floor? It will be reckoned unto me as a sin If I accept the service of Brahmans." The boy said, "This is my sister, and a Brahman has told us that unless you come to her wedding she will be widowed shortly after marriage. Our father and mother told us to go and bring you back with us. So, in order to make you pleased with us, we have been working as your servants." "Do not work for me any more," said Soma, "I shall gladly go to your wedding," She then called to her daughters-in-law and said, "I am going to this child's wedding. But if any one of our relations dies when I am away, do not burn his body until I come back." She went with the two Brahman children to the seashore. The wind was blowing, and the great waves were rolling in, and the foam was splashing over the rocks. But Soma took the boy under one arm and the girl under the other. She jumped far up into the sky and right over the seven seas, and when she got to the opposite shore she put the children down again. They led her to their father's house. Their mother Dhanvanti welcomed the washerwoman and fell at her feet to thank her for her coming. The youngest brother then went to Ujjain, and after making inquiries brought back a boy of suitable caste and age to be a husband for his sister. On an auspicious day the wedding was celebrated. But as the bridegroom and bride were throwing rice[14] over each other, the bridegroom fainted. He fell on the ground and lay there motionless. The little bride did not know what to do, she was so frightened. And all the grown-up people were almost as frightened as she was. But Soma, the washerwoman, stepped forward and said, "It is nothing, do not be afraid." She took some water in her hand and sprinkled it over herself. Now the secret of Soma's power was this:--

She had acquired great merit by observing every Monday the following practices: She would get up early, bathe, dress in silence, make various gifts to Brahmans, and then walk one hundred and eight times round a peepul tree. But now by sprinkling water over herself she had transferred the whole of her merit to Gunvanti. By this means the little bride had been able to restore her husband to life, and the wedding ceremony finished amidst the happiness of all. Soma then took leave to go, and started on her homeward journey. When she reached the seashore, the wind was blowing, and the great waves came rolling in, and the spray was splashing over the rocks. But now that she had given away all her merit to Gunvanti, she had none left by means of which she could jump across the seven seas. She sat down forlorn by the bank of a river. Then she got up, bathed in the water, and prayed to the god Vishnu. Next she took one hundred and eight sand-grains in her hand, and then walked one hundred and eight times round a peepul tree by the river's edge. Instantly her powers returned to her, and going back to the shore, she sprang into the heavens and over the seven seas and alighted close

[14] This is called the akshataropan.

to her own door. There all her little daughters-in-law ran out to meet her and cried, "O Mother-in-law, Mother-in-law, we have been watching for you. For while you were away your sons, your husband, and all your sons-in-law died. But just as you told us to do, we did not burn their corpses, but kept them in the house. And now they have all suddenly come back to life." Soma questioned the little daughters-in-law and learnt that her sons and husband and sons-in-law had all died at the very moment when she gave her merit to Gunvanti, and that they had come back to life precisely when she finished her one-hundred-and-eighth turn round the peepul tree. And they were all so glad to have Soma back with them again, and for ever such a long time afterwards she and her family lived happily together. And the Brahman in his joy at his son-in-law's recovery forgave his disobedient sons, and they too all lived happily together ever afterwards.

XIII

VASISHTA AND THE FOUR QUEENS

Once upon a time there was a town called Atpat. In it there ruled a king who had four wives. They were always quarrelling over the housework; so, in order to get some peace at home, the king himself divided the work between them. To the first queen he gave all the dairy work, to the second queen he gave all the cooking, to the third he gave the nursery, and he ordered the fourth to look after the royal wardrobe. At first all went well. But in a little while the first queen said to the third queen, "Why should you have charge of the nursery? Why should you not work in the dairy?" The second queen said to the fourth queen, "Why should I have to do all the cooking?" The third queen asked, "Why should I have always to look after the children?" And the fourth queen stamped her foot and said, "I *won't* look after the king's clothes." And all day long they quarrelled and screamed at each other, and the poor king was more uncomfortable than ever. His face grew sad and careworn, and, from the time he got up to the time he went to bed, he could think of nothing but the way that his four queens were squabbling with each other.

One day the rishi, or sage, Vasishta[15] paid the king a visit. The king prostrated himself before the great sage and gave him a throne to sit upon. Vasishta looked at the king's face and saw how sad and careworn it was. He asked the cause, and the king told him. Then the rishi rose, and the king went with him to the palace of the four queens. When they reached it, they called to the queens to come out. The rishi then asked them why they quarrelled. The first queen cried out, "Why should I have to do the dairy work?" And the second queen cried out, "Why should I be only a cook-woman?" And the third cried out, "Why should I have all the children to look after?" And the fourth cried out, "Why should I have all the bother of sorting out all the king's clothes?" The king said, "You must do these things because I ordered you to." But the queens did not mind a word that he said, and they all screamed together so loud that the king and the rishi had to put their fingers in their ears to save themselves from being deafened. For a while the rishi became absorbed in thought, and then he turned to the first queen and said, "You have been placed in charge of the dairy, have you not?" The first queen assented. "Then listen to me," said Vasishta. "In a former life you were a cow, and near the spot in the jungle where you used to graze was an altar to Shiva. And every day at noon you used to come and stand near it and let milk drop upon it. And, because in this way you honoured the god Shiva, you have in this life become one of the queens

[15] Vasishta was the family priest of King Dasaratha, father of Ramchandra. After death he became one of the stars in the constellation of the Great Bear.

of the king of Atpat. But you did not in your former life attain to full merit. So the god Shiva directed the king to place you in charge of his dairy, and the king conveyed the god's directions to you. You should therefore obey them, and you should honour the king as if he were Shiva himself. In this way you will attain to full merit and ascend to Shiva's heaven, Kailas." Vasishta then blessed the first queen. She prostrated herself before him, and, giving up all thought of quarrelling, went away and busied herself with her dairy work.

Then Vasishta turned to the second queen and asked, "What are you quarrelling about?" She replied, "Why should I be just a cook-woman?" The rishi thought for a while and said, "Lady, in a former life you were the wife of a poor Brahman, and you used to beg your food from door to door. But every Monday you used to fast, and whatever grain you begged that day you used to cook and offer to the god Shiva. And he was pleased with your devotion. Therefore in this life he made you one of the queens of Atpat. And because you cooked for the god Shiva, he directed the king to put you in charge of his kitchen. Therefore, obey the god's directions and give a great feast to all in Atpat. In this way you will gain the favour of Shiva, and he will take you with him to Kailas." Then he blessed the second queen, and she prostrated herself and went off quite cheerfully to cook the king's dinner.

The sage next turned to the third queen and asked, "What are you quarrelling about?" The queen answered, "Why should I do nothing but fiddle about the nursery?" Vasishta thought for a while and said, "In a former life, O Queen, you were a maid of a jungle tribe. Every Monday you used to fast yourself and offer the choicest fruits that you picked to the god Shiva. In return for them he has made you a queen, and he has entrusted the king's children to you. Therefore look after them and be kind to them, and in the end he will take you to live with him in Kailas." The rishi then blessed the third queen, and she prostrated herself before him. Then she ran off, her face all smiles, to play with the king's children.

Vasishta last of all turned to the fourth queen and said, "What are you quarrelling about?" She answered, "Why should I do nothing but look after the king's clothes?" The rishi said, "In a former life, O Queen, you were a kite that flew high up in the heavens. Beneath where you used to fly was an altar to Shiva, and every day at noon you would spread your wings over it and shade it from the sun's heat. So the god was pleased with you and in this life made you one of the queens of Atpat. As you spread your wings over Shiva's altar, so now a canopy hangs over your bed. And just as you served Shiva, now do service to the king, your husband. And you will thereby gain full merit and in the end reach Kailas." Then the rishi blessed her, and she went off quite gaily to attend to the king's clothes.

And the four queens never quarrelled any more, but lived happily ever afterwards with the king. And all little girls who hear this story should try to be as good as the queens were after Vasishta had cured them of their squabbling.

XIV

THE LAMPS AND THE KING'S DAUGHTER-IN-LAW

Once upon a time there was a town called Atpat. In it there lived a king who had one little daughter-in-law. Now she was a very greedy little girl, and one day when some sweetmeats were got ready for all the family she went quietly and ate them all up herself. Then she got very frightened, for she knew that, if the king knew what she had done, he would order her to be well slapped. So, when the family began asking where the sweetmeats were she said that the mice had eaten them. And then every one began abusing the mice, saying what horrid little wretches they were, and what a good thing it would be if the cat caught and ate them up. But, when the mice heard all this, they were very angry with the little daughter-in-law for bringing a false charge against them, and they all met together and vowed that they would be revenged on her. Some days later the king invited a guest to his house, and the same night the mice went into the little daughter-in-law's room and dragged out one of her bodices and put it across the guest's bed. Next morning the bodice was discovered in the stranger's bed, and the little daughter-in-law was utterly disgraced. Her father-in-law and all her brothers-in-law scolded her dreadfully, and at last the king drove her out of the house. Now it so happened that it had till then always been the work of the little daughter-in-law to look after the lamps in the king's palace. Every morning she used to rub them well and trim the wicks. She used to light them herself and neap the burners with sugar-candy, and on Divali[16] Day she used to worship them and make them suitable offerings. But, directly the little daughter-in-law was driven away, none of the lamps were any longer cared for. On the next Divali Day the king was returning from a hunt, and he camped under a tree. Suddenly he saw all the lamps in his town of Atpat come and settle on its branches. One lamp after another told what was happening in its house--when there had been a dinner party, what there had been to eat, who had been invited, how they themselves had been cared for, and what honours they had received on Divali Day. After all the other lamps had told their story, the big lamp from the king's palace began, "Brother lamps, I do not know how to tell you. For none among you is so wretched as I am. In former years I was the most fortunate of all the lamps in Atpat. No other lamp had such honours paid it as I had, and this year I have to drag out my days In unspeakable misery." All the other lamps tried to comfort it, and asked it how it was that ill-fortunc had overtaken it. "O brother lamps, how can I tell you?" repeated the big lamp. "I am the chief among the lamps that shine In the palace of the King of Atpat. One day the king's little daughter-in-law ate some sweetmeats and to save herself blamed

[16] Divali is the feast of lamps in the month of Kartih.

the mice. To revenge themselves, they in turn brought a false charge against her by putting her bodice on the bed of one of the king's guests. So she was disgraced and driven out of the house. And after she left ill-fortune came upon me. For every year it was she who worshipped me and paid me honour; and wherever she is I wish her well, and I give her my blessing." The king listened attentively to the talk between the lamps, and thus he learnt that his daughter-in-law was innocent. He went home and asked whether there was any other evidence against her besides her bodice. And when he learnt that there was none, and that no one had seen anything happen between her and the king's guest, he sent a messenger for her and had her brought home. And he begged her pardon for the past, and gave her full authority over all his household; and the king lived and ruled ever afterwards as wisely and as well as King Ramchandra of Ayodhya. And if any one brings a false charge against any of us, may the lamps save us as they did the king's little daughter-in-law.

XV

PARWATI AND THE PRIEST

Once upon a time there was a town called Atpat. In it there was a temple to the god Shiva. One day when Shiva and his wife Parwati were walking about they happened to come to this temple. They sat down there and began to play saripat.[17] After some time Parwati seeing a priest close by asked him who had won, she or Shiva. "Shiva," the priest replied. Parwati became very angry and cursed him, so that he became a leper, and the pains which overtook him were absolutely unendurable. One day a band of Apsaras[18] came down from heaven to the temple. They saw that the priest who lived in it was a leper, and they asked him the reason. He told them how Parwati had cursed him. They replied, "Do not be afraid; do as we tell you and you will get rid of your leprosy. Fast all next Monday, bathe that evening, worship the god Shiva, and then get half a pound of flour and mix it with treacle and ghee and eat it for dinner. But whatever you do, eat no salt all day. Do this for sixteen Mondays in succession, and on the seventeenth Monday get five pounds of flour, mix with it ghee and treacle, and offer it to Shiva inside this temple. Then divide it into three parts; leave one for the god, distribute a second among the Brahmans or give it to your cows, and take the third home to be eaten by you and your family." The Apsaras disappeared, and the priest followed their instructions and became quite well. Some time afterwards Shiva and Parwati came again to the temple. Parwati saw the priest cured of his leprosy and asked him how he had got rid of it. He told her exactly what he had done. She was very much surprised, and thought that if she did the same she might win back her son Kartakswami,[19] who had quarrelled with her and had run off in a rage. On the seventeenth Monday Kartakswami suddenly appeared, and both of them were reconciled. Later on, Kartakswami asked Parwati how she had brought him back, and Parwati told him. Now Kartakswami had a Brahman friend who had gone into a far-off country, and Kartakswami met him by accident shortly afterwards. He told the Brahman how the priest had cured himself of leprosy, and how he and Parwati had become reconciled. So the Brahman also practised the same rites for seventeen Mondays. He then set out for a distant country. As he travelled he came to a town. Now it happened that in that town arrangements were being made for the marriage of the king's daughter. Several princes had come from far-off countries to compete for her hand, and the king had erected a splendid pavilion for the royal betrothal. But he would not himself choose a prince to be his daughter's hus-

[17] Saripat is a kind of draughts.

[18] Apsaras are attendants on the gods.

[19] Kartakswami was really Parwati's step-son (see Preface).

band. He ordered that a garland should be placed on a she-elephant's trunk, and that the prince round whose neck the she-elephant threw the garland should be chosen to marry the king's daughter. But the she-elephant passed by all the princes in turn, until she came to where the Brahman stood. For he had come with the crowds of people to see the royal betrothal. Then the she-elephant stopped and put the garland round the Brahman's neck. The king ordered the Brahman to step forward, and he married him to his daughter. Some years later when the princess grew up, and she and the Brahman began to live together, she asked her husband by what merit he had succeeded in winning her for his wife, and he told her. And she in turn practised the same rites for seventeen Mondays. Nine months later a beautiful baby boy was born to her; and when he in turn grew up she told him the rites which she had practised to obtain him. And he in turn began to perform them. On the sixteenth Monday he set out for a journey. As he travelled in a distant country he came to a town over which ruled a king who had no son and only one daughter. The king had for a long time past been searching for a beautiful and virtuous young man, resolved when he found him to hand over to him his kingdom and marry him to his daughter. As the Brahman's son entered the town the king saw him and noticed on him all the marks of royal origin. So he summoned him to his house and married him to his daughter and seated him on his own throne. Now the next Monday was the seventeenth Monday since the Brahman's son had begun the rites which the Apsaras had told to the priest. That morning he got up and went to the temple and sent a message home to his wife that she should send him five sers of flour mixed with ghee and treacle. But the queen was too proud to do this. For she feared that the people in the street would laugh at her if she sent her husband five sers of flour mixed with ghee and treacle. So instead she sent him five hundred rupees in a plate. But because the flour and ghee and treacle were not sent, the king was unable to complete his ceremonial, and it was all spoilt. And the god Shiva instead of being pleased became very angry indeed. And he told the king that, if he kept the queen as his wife, he would lose his kingdom and die a beggar. Next day the king sent for his chief minister and told him what had happened. At first the minister said, "The kingdom belongs to the queen's father. If you drive her out your subjects will hate you." But the king replied, "Yes, but not to obey the god's command is a worse thing still." At last the minister agreed with the king, and the order went forth that the queen should be driven out of the city. So the queen was driven out and became quite poor and wandered along the road. At last she came to a distant town and lodged there with an old woman, who gave her food and drink. One day the old woman sent the queen out to sell fruit puddings. As she went into the bazaar a great wind came and carried off the fruit puddings. When she returned to the old woman's house, the queen told her what had happened, and the old woman drove her out of the house. Then she went and lodged with an oilman, who had great jars full of oil. But one day she went and looked inside the jars, and all the oil disappeared. So the oilman drove her off out of the house. The queen left the town and walked along until she came to a river with abundant water in it. But directly her eyes fell on the water, it all flowed away and left the water-bed quite dry. She then journeyed on until she came to a beautiful lake, but when her glance rested on the lake, it became full of worms, and the water began to stink. And, when the cowherds came as usual to water their cattle, the cattle would not drink the stinking water, and they had to go home thirsty. By chance a Gosavi, or holy man, came that way and saw the queen, and she told him her story. The holy man took her to his house and treated her as his own daughter, and she did her best to serve him faithfully. But, at whatever thing she looked, it would either disappear or become full of worms and maggots. At last the holy man searched for the cause of this by means of his inner knowledge. And thus he learnt that she had incurred the sin of spoiling the worship of Shiva, which the Apsaras had first taught the priest. Unless that sin were atoned for, her evil glance would never be purified. So the holy man prayed to the god Shiva, and the god was pleased with him; and when the holy man interceded with him on the queen's behalf, the god said that he would forgive her if she began and completed properly the rites which she had spoiled when her husband was performing them. The queen did so, and the god's anger vanished. Suddenly there rose in the heart of her husband, the king, a wish to see his queen, and he sent out messengers on every side to look for her. At last one of the messengers saw the queen in the holy man's hermitage and went back and told the king. The king was overjoyed, and, taking his chief minister with him, he journeyed to the hermitage. He threw himself at the holy man's feet and then loaded him with presents. And the holy man was pleased and said, "O King, I have treated your wife exactly as if she had been my own daughter. She has lived here just as if she had been in her father's house. Now take her with you back again and once more go through the marriage ceremony with her." The king consented, and both he and the queen prostrated themselves before the holy man, and then they both returned to Atpat. And they celebrated their home-coming with the greatest splendour. And the rest of the king's reign was as happy as possible. And we shall be just as happy if we honour Shiva like the King of Atpat did.

"She has lived here just as if she had been in her father's house"

XVI

THE RISHI AND THE BRAHMAN

Once upon a time there was a town called Atpat. In it there lived a Brahman. For many years he lived happily and cultivated his fields of rice and grain. But one day his wife gave up the observances imposed on her, and, as a result, the whole house was stained by her conduct, and pollution hung like a black cloud over it. Her husband should have driven her out, but he had not the heart to do so. So he, too, incurred the blame of his wife's sin. In course of time they died, and, as a punishment for their wickedness, the husband became in his next life a bullock, and the wife became a dog. But the gods so far relented as to find them a home in the house of their only son.

Now the son was a very pious man, who never failed in his religious rites. He worshipped the gods, gave memorial honours to his dead father, and welcomed to his house every Brahman who passed by. One year, on the anniversary of his father's death, he told his wife to prepare a milk-pudding in honour of the dead, and announced that he would invite Brahmans to partake of it. The wife was as pious as her husband and never failed to obey his commands. So she made a big milk-pudding, and she boiled vegetables and stewed fruits. But just as she had finished and was about to invite her husband and his Brahman guests to begin their feast, the dog saw that a snake had entered the grain-jar, which had not been properly shut, and that it had left its poisonous trail all over the grain from which the milk-pudding had been prepared. The dog at once realised that, if the Brahmans who had been invited to the memorial feast ate the poisoned grain, they would die, and that the sin of Brahman murder would be incurred by the host, her son. So she suddenly rushed up and put her foot right into the middle of the milk-pudding. The son's wife was very angry. She threw a red-hot coal at the dog with such skill that it dropped on to the middle of her back and burnt a big hole in it. Then the son's wife cooked a fresh milk-pudding and fed the Brahmans. But she was so cross with the dog that she would not give her the smallest possible scrap. So the poor dog remained hungry all day. When night fell she went to the bullock who had been her husband and began to howl as loudly as she could. The bullock asked her what the matter was. She told him how she had seen that a snake had poisoned the grain, and how, to prevent the Brahmans dying and her son incurring the sin of their death, she had put her paw into the middle of the milk-pudding; how her daughter-in-law had been angry and had burnt a hole in her back with a live coal, and how her back hurt so that she did not know what to do. The bullock answered, "You are suffering for the pollution with which you darkened our house in a former life, and, because I let you remain in the house and touched you, I too am suffering, and I have become a bullock. Only to-day my son fastened me to his plough, tied up my mouth, and beat me, I too have, like you, had nothing to eat all day. Thus all my son's memorial services are useless." Now the son happened to be passing by the stable and heard this conversation. He at once fetched the bullock some grass and the dog some food, and he brought them both water to drink; and then he went to bed very sad at heart. Next morning he got up early and went into a dark forest until at last he came to the hermitage of a rishi. He prostrated himself before the rishi, who asked him why he was so sad. The Brahman's son said, "I am sad because my father has been born again as a bullock and my mother as a dog. Pray tell me how I can get their release," The rishi said, "There is only one way to help them. You must worship the seven sages who have their home in the Great Bear."[20] And he told the Brahman's son the ceremonies which he should observe, and how he should worship the seven sages continually every month of Bhadrapad, or September, for seven years. The Brahman's son obeyed the rishi, and at the end of the seven years a fiery chariot came down from heaven. The bullock suddenly became a handsome man, and the dog became a handsome woman. They both seated themselves in the chariot and were carried off to live with the sages who have their home for ever in the Great Bear.

[20] The Indians do not associate the Great Bear constellation with a bear, but they believe it to be the habitation of seven rishis. The seven rishis vary in different works. In the Mahabharat the names given are Marichi, Atri, Angiras, Pulaha, Kratu, Pulatya, and Vasishta.

XVII

THE KING AND THE WATER-GODDESSES

Once upon a time there was a town called Atpat. Over it there ruled a king. One day he founded a new village, and close by he built a village tank. But no matter how hard he tried he could not get it filled with water. So he prayed to the water-goddesses to help him, and the water-goddesses were pleased and said, "O King, O King, sacrifice to us the eldest son of your daughter-in-law, and the tank will fill with water." The king heard it and went home very troubled. He was ready to sacrifice his grandson; for though he loved the boy, yet he knew that the life of one was less than the welfare of many. But he knew that his daughter-in-law would never agree. At last he thought of a trick. He went up to her and said, "Daughter-in-law, it is a long time since you went to see your parents. You had better go and pay them a visit and leave your eldest boy behind. I shall look after him here." The daughter-in-law consented and went to visit her parents, leaving her son behind. The king waited for a favourable day and then bathed and anointed his grandson. He gave a feast in his honour and covered his body with costly jewelry. He then took him into the middle of the pond and made him lie down on a bed and told him not to stir. The water-goddesses were pleased, and a great mass of water suddenly rushed into the tank, and it was filled right up to the brink. After a time the daughter-in-law came back from her father's house and brought her brother with her. They asked where her son was, but they could get no information. Whenever they asked the king, he did nothing but say how the water had come into the tank, and what a beautiful tank it was, and how happy it would make all the villagers. At last the daughter-in-law guessed what had happened, and when the seventh day of the bright half of the month of Shravan, or August, came round, she and her brother went to the edge of the tank and began to worship the water-goddesses. She took a cucumber leaf, and on it she placed some curds and rice. Next she mixed with them some butter and a farthing's worth of betel-nut. Then she told her brother to pray, "O Goddess, Mother of All, if any one of our family is drowned in the tank please give him back to us." He did so and then threw the offering into the lake. Then they both turned to go home. But as she was turning homewards, she felt some one pull her by the legs. She looked down and saw that it was her missing son. When she saw him she dragged him with all her might to the bank, and then she and her brother walked home with him. When the king heard that she was coming, together with her missing son, he wondered greatly, and going to her he fell at her feet and said, "O my daughter, I offered your son to the water-goddesses; how has he come back again?" She said,

"I worshipped the water-goddesses and made offerings to them. Then my son came out of the water, and I lifted him up and drew him to the shore." The king was overjoyed and showed the greatest favour to his daughter-in-law. And she and her little son lived happily ever afterwards.

XVIII

THE LID OF THE SACRED CASKET

Once upon a time there was a town called Atpat. In it there lived a Brahman who had two twin sons. While they were still quite young, the twins' parents died, and their relatives stole from them all their property and then turned them out of the house. The twins wandered along until they came to a town. It was then noon, and the boys were weary with walking and were tortured with hunger and thirst. As they entered the town, a Brahman came out of his door to throw food to the crows. He saw the two boys and called them in, fed them, and then made them tell him their story. When he heard it he resolved to provide for them, and he lodged them in his house and taught them to recite the Vedas. On Lalita Panchmi Day the Brahman began to perform certain ceremonies. His pupils asked him why he did so. The sage replied that by doing so one could attain to wealth, knowledge, and to the wish of one's heart. The boys begged him to instruct them, and they quickly learnt how to worship the goddess Parwati. Not long afterwards the Brahman provided them with wives, and they returned to their own city, acquired wealth, and were very happy. A year or two later the twins separated. But the elder was a wise boy and never forgot to worship the goddess Parwati on Lalita Panchmi Day. So he retained the riches which he had gained. But the younger was foolish and forgot all about it, so the goddess began to dislike him, and he lost all his money. And at last he became so poor that he and his wife had to give up their house and go and live on the charity of his elder brother. One day the elder brother's wife spoke so crossly and said such nasty things to the younger twin, that he felt that he could not stay in the house any longer. And he remembered then that of recent years he had entirely forgotten to worship Parwati. He felt very penitent, and he decided that somehow or other he would win back the goddess's favour. Taking his wife with him, he left his brother's house and journeyed to a distant country. At last he came near a town, and, meeting a cowherd, the younger twin asked him what its name was. The cowherd said, "The town is called Upang." "Who is the king?" asked the younger twin. The cowherd replied, "He also is called Upang." The wanderer then asked whether there was any place where he and his wife could lodge. The cowherd told him that in the town there was a temple of Parwati, and close to it was a rest-house where the wanderer and his wife could lodge. The cowherd directed them to the rest-house. And before lying down the younger twin worshipped Parwati in the temple and begged her pardon for his previous neglect. Parwati felt sorry for him, and that night she appeared to him in a dream. She told him to go to King Upang's palace and to beg from him the lid of the sacred casket in which the accessories of worship were kept. He should, thereafter, always pray to it, and in the end he would come by his heart's desire. The younger twin woke up, and the same morning he went to King Upang's palace and begged from him the lid of the sacred casket in which were kept the accessories of worship. The king at first refused, but when the younger twin told the king of his dream the king consented. The Brahman took the lid home, worshipped it, and, just as the goddess had foretold, he came by his heart's desire. Property and happiness returned, and a year later his wife bore him a daughter. As the years passed the little girl grew up. One day she took the lid of the sacred casket and went with some playmates to play and bathe by the bank of a river. Suddenly the corpse of a Brahman came floating by. Seeing it, the little girl took the lid of the casket and for fun began to splash water on it. Such was the power of the sacred lid, that the corpse instantly became alive again and became a Brahman, tall as a tree and beautiful as the sun. The little girl fell in love with him on the spot and told him that he must become her husband. "But," said the Brahman, "how shall I manage it?" The little girl said, "Come home with me at dinner-time, take as usual water[21] in your hand, but do not sip it. Then my daddy will ask you, 'Bhatji, Bhatji, why do you not sip the water in your hand?' You must reply, 'I am ready to dine if you marry me to your daughter. If you will not, I shall get up and go away.' Then he will consent to our marriage." The Brahman agreed, and he went home with the little girl, and everything happened as she had planned. To prevent the Brahman from getting up without any food, the little girl's father agreed to their marriage. When a favourable day came they were married, and when she was old enough the little girl went to her husband's house. As she went she carried off the lid of the sacred casket of King Upang. But, because it had gone, her father lost all his wealth and fell once more into the greatest poverty. His wife went to her daughter's house and asked for it back, but she refused to give it up. The wife was very angry and every day began to hate her son-in-law more and more. But for him, as she thought, the little girl would never have married and would not have stolen the lid of the sacred casket. One day the wife met her son-in-law on the road, and she gave him such a fearful slap in the face that he instantly fell on the ground and became a corpse again. His mother-in-law then-snatched from him the lid of the casket, which he happened to have in his hand, and ran away home. There he lay until the little girl, his wife, began to search for him. When she found him she prayed to the goddess, and by her aid and by means of the merit which she had acquired by worshipping the lid of the casket while she had it, she restored her husband to life. But the twin and his wife went on becoming poorer and poorer. And at last they went back to his brother's house and asked him why it was that the younger twin was always losing his wealth as fast as he gained it. The elder brother listened to the whole story and then he said, "I do not wonder at it. First you lost the lid of the casket, then, in order to get it back, your wife killed a Brahman. Your only chance now is to worship Parwati harder than ever, and perhaps in the end you may recover your good estate." So the younger brother went home and worshipped Parwati with greater vigour than ever. And at last she relented and gave him her blessing.

[21] Aposhani. This is the water which a Brahman sips from his hand before and after his meal.

He recovered his wealth and came by all that his heart desired. And he and his wife lived happily ever afterwards.

XIX

THE BRAHMAN WIFE AND HER SEVEN SONS

Once upon a time there was a town called Atpat. In it there lived a poor Brahman who used always to perform Shradh or memorial ceremonies to his father on the last day of the month of Shravan. When performing these ceremonies he always invited other Brahmans to dine. But it so happened that on every last day of the month of Shravan,[22] from the day of his father's death onwards, his daughter-in-law gave birth to a little boy. And just as the Brahmans had begun to enjoy their dinner, the child would die. So all the Shradh ceremonies had to cease, and the poor Brahmans had to be sent away feeling most dreadfully hungry. This happened regularly for six years. But, when the seventh little boy was born only to die just as his guests were beginning to enjoy their dinner, the poor Brahman lost all patience. He took the newly-born child and placed it in his daughter-in-law's lap and then drove her out of the house and into the jungle. The poor woman walked along until she came to a great, dark forest. In it she met the wife of a hobgoblin,[23] who asked, "Lady, Lady, whose wife are you, and why do you come here? Run away as quickly as you can. For, if my husband the hobgoblin sees you, he will tear you to pieces and gobble you up." The poor woman said she was the daughter-in-law of a Brahman, and explained how every year she had given birth to a son on the last day of Shravan, how it had died in the middle of the Shradh feast, and how at last her father-in-law had put the child in her lap and had driven her from home and into the forest. The hobgoblin's wife repeated, "If you value your life at all, go away." The Brahman woman began to cry, until at last the hobgoblin's wife had pity on her and said, "Do not be afraid; walk a little way until you come to an altar to the god Shiva, Close by is a bel[24] tree; climb into it and hide among the branches. To-night the serpent-maidens from Patâla and the wood-nymphs, together with a train of seven demon Asuras,[25] will come and worship at the altar. After making their offerings to the god, they will call out, 'Is there any uninvited guest present to whom we can make a gift?' You must then call out in reply, 'Yes,

[22] Shravan corresponds roughly with August. The death of the child nullified all the virtue of the Shradh feast, which had at once to be stopped.

[23] Zhoting is really the unquiet ghost of a Musulman, but hobgoblin is probably a sufficiently close translation.

[24] A tree sacred to Shiva.

[25] The Asuras, who are now reckoned petty demons, had once upon a time a much higher position. They are the same as Ahura-Magda, the Jupiter of the Iranians. The latter, curiously enough, degraded the Devas or Hindu Gods to the subordinate place of demons. (Cf. Rawlinson's *Bactria*, page 21.)

I am here.' They will see you and question you, and you must tell them all your story." The poor Brahman woman agreed. She walked on until she came to the god Shiva's altar. She climbed into the branches of the bel tree. She remained there until midnight came. Suddenly the serpent-maidens from Patâla and the wood-nymphs, accompanied by a train of seven demon Asuras, came and worshipped at the altar. After making offerings to the god they called out, "Is there any uninvited guest present to whom we can make a gift?" The Brahman woman at once climbed down the bel tree and called out in answer, "Yes, I am here," The serpent-maidens from Pâtala and the wood-nymphs, greatly surprised, asked her who she was, and she told them all her story. Then the serpent-maidens of Pâtala and the wood-nymphs ordered their train of demon Asuras to go and search for the seven sons of the Brahman woman. The seven demon Asuras spurred their horses and rode off in all directions. In a little time the giant captain of the demon guards rode up carrying in his arms the body of a little boy of six. Then another rode up carrying the body of a little boy of five. And four others rode up carrying a little boy of four, a little boy of three, a little boy of two, and a little boy only one year old. Last of all the seventh demon Asura rode up with a newly-born baby boy. The demons placed the bodies in front of the serpent-maidens from Patâla and of the wood-nymphs. And first of all the little boy of six came to life and got up and ran to his mother. Next the little boy of five, and then the little boy of four, and then the little boy of three came to life and ran to their mother. Then the little boy of two came to life and got up, but he could only walk to his mother. Next the little one-year-old boy came to life, but he could not get up, so he lay on his back and kicked up his legs. And last of all the newly-born baby came to life, but he could not even kick up his legs. And they were all delighted to see their mother, and she was overjoyed to have all her sons again. But the serpent-maidens from Patâla and the wood-nymphs warned her that she must pray to the sixty-four Yoginis, the attendants who wait on Durga, the Goddess of Death, or else her children would be snatched from her again. And they told her to pray her hardest, for her prayer had to travel down to the depths of Hell. So the Brahman woman prayed her hardest to the sixty-four Yoginis, and then she prostrated herself before the serpent-maidens from Patâla, and the wood-nymphs, and their train of demon Asuras. And then she took the little one-year-old boy on her hip, and the newly-born baby boy in her arms, and she walked with her other five sons to the village. When the villagers saw her coming they ran and said to the Brahman, "Bhatji, Bhatji, your daughter-in-law is coming back home." And the Brahman became very angry and vowed that he would drive her away again. So he watched for her coming. But first of all he saw walking towards his house a little boy of six, and then a little boy of five, and then a little boy of four, and then two other little boys of three and two. Last of all he saw his daughter-in-law with a one-year-old boy on her hip and a newly-born baby in her arms. He rose and fetched a cauldron of water and two handfuls of rice from his house. And he waved his hands filled with rice round the heads of his daughter-in-law and of all her children, and last of all he washed their feet. In this way he welcomed back to his house his grandchildren and their mother. And he made her tell him all her story; and she, and her children, and the Brahman spent the rest of their lives in great peace and perfect happiness.

XX

THE GOLDEN TEMPLE

Once upon a time there was a town called Atpat. In it there reigned a king who had four daughters-in-law. He loved three of them very dearly, but the fourth, who was an ugly little girl, he did not like at all. To the three daughters-in-law he gave nice food and fine clothes. But to the ugly little daughter-in-law he gave nothing but scraps from his table and thick, coarse clothes to wear. He would not even let her sleep inside the house, but made her sleep in the stable and look after the cows. The poor ugly daughter-in-law grew so unhappy that, when the first Monday in Shravan[26] came, she ran out of the palace, and out of the town, and then away as fast as her fat little legs would carry her. At last she went and hid herself in the woods. Now it so happened that that very day a band of serpent-maidens[27] had come up from Patala. After wandering through the forest and bathing in the running streams, they had joined a bevy of wood-nymphs and were coming in her direction. At first she was too terrified to say a single word. But at last she asked, "Ladies, ladies, where are you going?" "To the temple of Shiva," they replied, "to worship the god. For by doing that, one wins the love of one's husband, one obtains children, and one comes by the wish of one's heart." When the ugly daughter-in-law heard that by doing what the serpent-maidens and the wood-nymphs were about to do she could win love for herself, she at once thought that in this way she, too, might win the love of her father-in-law. So she told the serpent-maidens of Patala and the wood-nymphs that she would go with them. They went deeper and deeper into the forest until at last they came to a temple of the god Shiva. There the serpent-maidens and the wood-nymphs offered to the god rice, betel-nut, incense, flowers, and the leaves of the bel tree. The ugly little daughter-in-law did just as they did. And when she had finished she cried out, "O God Shiva, please, please vouchsafe my prayer also, and make my father-in-law and my mother-in-law, my brothers-in-law and my sisters-in-law like me as much as they now dislike me." That evening she went home and fasted, and all the scraps which they threw to her from the king's table she gave to her favourite cow. And then she sat by herself and prayed to the god Shiva. The following Monday she once more ran out of the palace and out of the town and into the woods as fast as her fat little legs would carry her. There she met again the serpent-maidens of Patâla and the bevy of wood-nymphs and went with them to the temple of Shiva

[26] Shravan = August.

[27] Nag-kanya. These are the maidens of the race of the Nagas, who are said to have sprung from Kadru, wife of Kasyapa. One of them, Ulupi, married the hero Arjuna. They live in Patâla, the lowest of the seven underground regions.

in the distant heart of the forest. The first time the serpent-maidens and the wood-nymphs had given her the incense and the flowers, the rice and the betel-nut, and the leaves of the bel tree, with which to perform her worship. But they had told her that the next time she must bring them herself. So when she ran away on the second Monday in Shravan she brought with her incense and flowers, rice and betel-nut and bel-tree leaves, and after offering them and some sesamums to the god she once more prayed, "O God Shiva, please, please grant my prayer and make my father-in-law and my mother-in-law, my brothers-in-law and my sisters-in-law like me as much as they now dislike me." Then she went home and fasted, and giving all her dinner to her favourite cow she sat by herself and prayed to Shiva. That evening the king asked her who the god was whom she was honouring, and where he lived. The ugly little daughter-in-law replied, "Afar off my god lives, and the roads to him are hard, and the paths to him are full of thorns. Where snakes abound and where tigers lie in wait, there is his temple." The third Monday in Shravan, the ugly little daughter-in-law again started from the palace with her flowers and incense, her betel-nut and bel leaves, her rice and sesamum, in order to meet the serpent-maidens of Patâla and the bevy of wood-nymphs, and with them to worship the god in the hidden depths of the forest. This time the king and her other male relatives followed her and said to her, "Ugly little daughter-in-law, take us with you and show us your god." But the temple of Shiva was ever so far from the king's palace. The ugly daughter-in-law did not mind, for she was used to cruel treatment. She had also walked to the temple twice before, and her feet had got as hard as two little stones. But the king and his relatives were tired to death; and their feet swelled up to the size of an elephant's, and they became as full of thorns as the back of a porcupine. And they muttered to each other, "How on earth does that ugly little daughter-in-law manage to walk as she does through the heart of the forest?" The ugly daughter-in-law at last felt sorry for them. She prayed to the god Shiva to build a temple near at hand. The god consented, and, with the help of the serpent-maidens of Patâla and of the wood-nymphs, he created suddenly a beautiful temple all of pure, yellow gold. Its pillars were studded with jewels, and the jars in it were all of crystal. In the middle there rose from the ground an altar to the god Shiva. And last of all the god revealed himself to the king and his companions in all his glory and splendour. For a moment only they saw him; and then he vanished. The king and his companions stared, too astonished to move or speak. But the ugly little daughter-in-law prostrated herself and offered to the god flowers and incense. Then she cried out, "O God Shiva, please, please vouchsafe my prayer and make my father-in-law and my mother-in-law, my brothers-in-law and my sisters-in-law like me as much as they now dislike me." When the king heard her prayer his heart softened to her, and he spoke kindly to her and gave her jewelry and trinkets. In a little while he took off his turban and, placing it on a peg, walked out to look at a lovely lake which, unnoticed by any one before, now stretched out close by the temple. And behind him strolled out his companions. But when they had gone out of sight, the beautiful golden temple by the lake vanished for ever. After looking at the lake the king came back to fetch his turban which he had left in the temple. But he could not find the beautiful temple all of pure, yellow gold, with its jewel-studded pillars and its crystal

"The god revealed himself to the king and his companions in all his glory and splendour"

jars. The king asked the little daughter-in-law the cause. She said nothing, but straightway walked deeper into the forest. And the king and his companions, although weary to death, followed her. At last they came to the temple where she had worshipped, together with the serpent-maidens from Patâla and the bevy of wood-nymphs. It was a tiny temple, and inside it there was a rough altar. At the foot of the altar lay the flowers which the ugly daughter-in-law had offered to the god, and close by on a peg hung the turban left by the king. Again the king asked his daughter-in-law the meaning of what had happened. She replied, "This temple that you see is my own poor little temple. But, because of my prayers, the god Shiva showed himself to you in the beautiful temple, all of pure, yellow gold, with its jewel-studded pillars and its crystal jars." When the king heard her reply, he grew more pleased than ever with the daughter-in-law whom formerly he had so disliked. And because the god had revealed himself at her prayer, the king, to do her honour, sent for his royal palanquin and had her carried home in state. And the ugly little daughter-in-law became out of the four the king's favourite. And he was so much nicer to her than he was to his other three daughters-in-law that they became as jealous as cats. But the king and the ugly little daughter-in-law did not mind them the least little bit. And they both lived happily ever afterwards.

THE END.

Printed by Libri Plureos GmbH in Hamburg,
Germany

9 789358 007428